T0176207

FLORENCE

Like a Local

FLORENCE
Like a Local

BY THE PEOPLE WHO CALL IT HOME

Contents

NIGHTLIFE

OUTDOORS

meet the locals

VINCENZO D'ANGELO

Vincenzo has been in a full-time relationship with Florence since moving to study in 2010. Between working as a digital project manager and writing, he's finding new aperitivo and dinner spots (the hunt for which he considers his favourite sport) and advocating for LGBTQIA+ rights.

MARY GRAY

When Mississippi-born Mary came to Florence to study a decade ago, she failed to find reasons to leave. She's kept busy as a freelance journalist and a media studies lecturer, but always finds time to scour vintage fairs and host dinner parties.

PHOEBE HUNT

Born in London, Phoebe moved to Florence for a summer and never left. She's been an au pair, done a stint cooking in a Tuscan restaurant and posed for paintings, but she mostly works as a travel journalist. Find her practising her Italian at the market or people-watching in the piazza.

Florence

WELCOME TO THE CITY

There's a timeless quality to life in Florence. In the city's centuries-old streets, tradition is honoured and guarded with full force. You'll find goldsmiths clinking metal in historic workshops, chefs cooking up family recipes that have been passed through the generations and baristas serving strong coffees in a way little changed for decades. Above all, though, Florence is the birthplace of the Renaissance – a living museum of elegant palaces and stately statues. Here, it's easy to forget not only the day but the decade.

Are Florentines stuck in the past? No, they're simply proud of their heritage. You only have to glance at Dante's statue standing tall in Santa Croce for a local to launch into a spiel on the home of the modern Italian language (spoiler, it's Florence), or raise an eyebrow at *lampredotto* – the city's traditional tripe dish – to cause mortal offence. Yet for all their devotion to the city's history, Florentines very much live in the present, embodying *la dolce vita* with full force. You'll see it in the hours spent people-watching in the piazza, the drawn-out dinners where stories are swapped and the ritualistic *passeggiata* through the cobbled, narrow lanes. Rushing anywhere and anything is simply impossible, and isn't that the endless allure of Italy: a life lived slowly, sweetly and fully?

Of course, any trip to Florence is sure to include a visit to the Uffizi or a sunset stroll up to Piazzale Michelangelo. But this book shows you that the real delight is in the stops you'll make along the way. It's the impulsive amble through a riverside flea market or the *aperitivo* at an un-signposted bar that make you fall in love with this city. So, go on, give into the *no ansia* philosophy and enjoy the beauty of the moment – it's pretty hard not to in Florence.

Liked by the locals

"Florence isn't about queuing for the Uffizi or ticking off churches. For me, it's a joyful morning cappuccino in the sun, a spontaneous evening *passeggiata* with friends, and that magic couple of minutes when you pause, look up and take it all in."

PHOEBE HUNT, TRAVEL JOURNALIST

Florence is as irresistible on a frosty morning as a balmy afternoon. From spring picnics to winter fashion shows, each season has its own appeal.

Florence
THROUGH THE YEAR

SPRING

TRADITIONAL FESTIVITIES
Pulling Florence out of hibernation are joyous celebrations. Carnevale kicks off in February with colourful parades, while Easter Sunday sees locals line the streets to glimpse a rocket in the shape of a dove being zip-lined into Piazza Duomo.

WONDERFUL WOMEN
International Women's Day in March coincides with Italy's very own Festa della Donna. Locals give bouquets of yellow mimosa flowers to the women in their lives, and bakeries sell themed cakes.

FLORENCE IN BLOOM
Fresh flowers sprout almost overnight in April: irises bloom at the Iris Garden,

wisteria takes over the Bardini gardens and roses paint the Rose Garden, resulting in the first picnics of the year.

SUMMER

FOOTBALL FEVER
The summer heats up with the Calcio Storico in June, a historic local football match where elbowing is encouraged. Fans get to Piazza Santa Croce early to watch amateurs fight for the trophy, but most people join the revelry after, when fireworks dazzle over the city.

ALFRESCO NIGHTS
Though *gelato* provides some sweet relief, June and July days are almost too hot to function. Come night, however, the cooler air pulls linen-wearing locals

outside, with crowds pitching up to dine on the piazza, and enjoy outdoor cinema nights and music festivals.

SLOWING DOWN
Florence falls into a slumber for the first two weeks of August, when most locals head to the seaside (Forte dei Marmi being a favourite) and many restaurants and bars close. It's all in aid of *Ferragosto*: a holiday on 15 August dedicated to rest.

AUTUMN
COCKTAIL O'CLOCK
September sees relaxed locals return to the city, ready to share summer stories and show off their tans. Florence Cocktail Week offers the perfect chance, when the bars closed in August reopen with mixology events and late-night parties.

CULTURAL PICKINGS
Though days are still mild, film festivals, new exhibitions and the start of the opera season tempt Florentines indoors.

HARVEST TIME
With the season of dinner parties upon them, locals look forward to the harvest, when markets overflow with bounties:

tomatoes in September, porcini mushrooms in November. Wine-making is also in full flow at Chianti vineyards, and many locals lend a hand picking grapes (in return for a few bottles).

WINTER
COSY TRATTORIAS
Florentines love a fireside dinner with friends to keep warm in the chillier months. Nights are spent lingering over winter dishes like *ribollita* soup and wild boar *ragù*, washed down with sweet wine.

FESTIVE CHEER
The switching on of the Christmas lights in early December is always a big deal, with a life-size singing nativity scene in Piazza della Signoria. The fun extends until Epiphany on 6 January, when La Befana (often compared to Santa) fills children's stockings with sweets.

MEN'S FASHION
Pitti Uomo, one of the biggest events in the men's fashion world, draws in fashionistas every January. As well as the iconic runway show, expect glamorous parties and male models strolling the streets in *haute couture*.

There's an art to being a Florentine, from the dos and don'ts of ordering a coffee to navigating the narrow streets. Here's a breakdown of all you need to know.

Florence
KNOW-HOW

For a directory of health and safety resources, safe spaces and accessibility information, turn to page 186. For everything else, read on.

EAT
Mealtimes are important in Florence. Breakfasts are a quick affair, while lunch – between 12 and 3pm – is time to indulge, be it a sandwich on a piazza or a sit-down meal in a trattoria. Dinner starts at around 8pm and isn't to be rushed, so book ahead to claim a table. Oh, and in a city that loves meat, tell the chef if you're veggie or vegan.

DRINK
Italy runs on coffee, and Florence is no exception. A morning cappuccino is drunk quickly at the bar (it's cheaper than sitting) and is never ordered after 12pm – most baristas will refuse to serve one. Another no-no is hogging tables: traditional cafés aren't modelled around nursing coffees and using laptops.

The rules are more relaxed when it comes to alcohol. At lunch, you're usually served a carafe of wine with your meal; locals think nothing of heading back to work after a glass or two of red. Around 6pm, everyone enjoys *aperitivo* – Italian "happy hour" – before dinner, and an *amaro digestivo* after the meal.

SHOP
Per favore and *grazie* will get you a long way when shopping – while the younger generation mostly speak English, those over 50 often don't, and will appreciate your efforts to speak Italian. As you know, lunch is to be indulged, so smaller shops tend to close from 12:30 to 3pm. Daily food markets are often only open until lunchtime, so get your dinner plans

sorted early to buy the best produce. Haggling is essential in touristy markets like San Lorenzo, but rare elsewhere.

ARTS & CULTURE

Museums and galleries aren't free (unless it's the first Sunday of the month), but they're some of the world's best, and it's worth pre-booking to avoid endless queues. Be mindful of artifacts inside – don't touch, and watch where you sit.

For the theatre, glam up and arrive in plenty of time. In churches, shorts and strappy tops are a no-go; if you can, a small donation is always appreciated.

NIGHTLIFE

The golden rule of nights out is not to peak too early. Locals savour negronis rather than downing shots, and aren't impressed at those getting inebriated. Pace yourself and join the locals in the unspoken art of *aperitivo*: one drink, one snack. On summer nights people congregate in piazzas from 11pm, and can easily stay chatting until dawn – unless they move on to a club that is, with queues forming around midnight.

OUTDOORS

Italian life centres around the outdoors, where afternoon *passeggiate* (strolls) and people-watching on the piazza are pastimes. Be mindful of where you perch to eat and drink, though: in busy squares, police are cracking down on sitting and drinking on the steps to churches. You'll get a *multa* (fine) if you ignore them.

Keep in mind

Here are some other tips and tidbits that will help you fit in like a local.

» **Carry cash** Most places accept contactless payments over €5, but some markets are cash-only.

» **Tipping** Tips aren't required, but rounding up to the nearest euro is always welcome. Some places add *coperto* (table service charges) to your bill.

» **Smoke outside** A lot of Italians smoke, but lighting up indoors is banned, so save it for when you're on a café terrace or the piazza.

» **Stay hydrated** There are plenty of still – and some sparkling – water fountains around the city so bring a reusable bottle.

GETTING AROUND

Florence's small city centre is mostly contained within the old city walls and divided in two by the river Arno. The northern portion is home to the most famous sights, while the south – known as the Oltrarno, which literally means "across the Arno" – is more artsy.

Areas are referred to by their piazza, which tend to take their name from the closest church, cathedral or street name. Still, the limits between neighbourhoods are subjective, and many locals call a handful of areas "centre". Addresses can be tricky too, with older streets running a dual numbering system, with red *(rosso)* signs for businesses – signified by an "r" after the house number – and black *(nero)* for private residences.

Disoriented? To make your life easier, we've provided what3words addresses for each sight in this book, meaning you can quickly pinpoint exactly where you're heading with ease.

On foot

Compact enough to explore on foot, Florence is a place to get joyfully lost down winding streets. *Passeggiate* – or strolls – are a way of life, especially along the Arno at sunset, and the pace of walking is slow and leisurely at all times. That said, if you're on a narrow street and need to check a what3words location, wait to reach a wider street to stop – foot traffic jams are best avoided, *grazie*. If you get lost, look for the Duomo: it'll never be too far away. Oh, and while the temptation to wear your sparkling new brogues or cute heels might be hard to resist, remember most streets are cobbled and can be steep.

On wheels

Despite being a tiny city, locals cycle everywhere they can, ringing their bells in exasperation as they weave around dawdling pedestrians. Cyclists don't always obey traffic lights or one-way systems, but this is the one time we'll advise you not to follow the locals. Roads can also be narrow and visibility poor, so always wear a helmet and keep lights on.

Sergio Bianchi are the coolest bikes to be seen riding, made in Tuscany and available to hire from Tuscany Cycle. For shorter rides, download the RideMovi app and pick up a MoBike: they're in abundance around the centre and can be left anywhere. If you're heading to the hilly suburbs or cycling on a hot day, we suggest you hire an electric bike through the RideMovi app.
www.ridemovi.com
www.tuscanycycle.com

By public transport

Given how accessible everything in the centre is by foot or bike, locals tend to avoid public transport unless leaving the city. Florence is well positioned for trains to major Italian cities, leaving from Firenze Santa Maria Novella.

Within the city, the Tramvia system takes you to the outskirts, including Novoli and Scandicci. Buses can be unreliable, with timetables rarely up to date, so be prepared to wait if you're travelling to Fiesole or into Chianti.

Tram and bus tickets can be bought in bulk from any local *tabacchi* (look out for the blue T). Make sure you scan your ticket when you get on to validate it, to avoid fines by heavy-handed officials.

By car and taxi

Chaotic one-way systems and tricky parking mean cars tend to be the reserve of those who live in the hills or suburbs. If you're visiting Chianti, it's another story – the winding roads are some of the most iconic in Europe, so it's worth renting a vintage Fiat from Tuscany By Car to explore the area.

Taxis run all night, picking people up from airports and clubs outside of the centre. They aren't cheap, though, so it's best to use them for long trips only.
www.tuscany-by-car.it

Download these

We recommend you download these apps to help you get about the city.

WHAT3WORDS
Your geocoding friend
A what3words address is a simple way to communicate any precise location on earth, using just three words. ///raced.mammal.oath, for example, is the code for the bronze replica of Michelangelo's *David* at the Piazzale Michelangelo viewpoint. Simply download the free what3words app, type a what3words address into the search bar, and you'll know exactly where to go.

TRENITALIA
Your transport service
Let's face it: you're more likely to use public transport to move around outside of the city than within it.

High-speed rail services are provided from Florence to cities outside the region by Trenitalia, and the official app lets you reserve allocated seating and book tickets months in advance.

Florence is a patchwork of small neighbourhoods, each with its own character and community. Here we take a look at some of our favourites.

Florence
NEIGHBOURHOODS

Campo di Marte

Formerly a training ground for the army, this residential area retains a team spirit today. The city's "sports neighbourhood" is home to rugby fields, an athletics track and the Artemio Franchi stadium, where fans cheer on the beloved ACF Fiorentina football team. {map 6}

Duomo

Only official maps call this area its historic name, San Giovanni. Locals, rather, refer to the small patch where the most famed landmarks lie as the "Duomo area". Sure, this historic heart has a touristy reputation, but hidden cafés, artisanal shops and the realization that they're in the cradle of the Renaissance can't keep locals away. {map 1}

Le Cure

Named after the washer-women (the "*cure*") who would do their laundry in the Mugnone river, Le Cure is suburban life at its best. North of Florence's old city walls, this is where long-standing residents have resided for generations and young families settle down. Non-residents still pass through for the iconic market, cute bakeries and fantastic wine bars. {map 6}

Novoli

Once the centre of the steel industry, Novoli in the northwest has undergone many renovations to turn it into a residential district. It's a student stronghold, home to the social sciences centre of the University of Florence and a handful of lesser-known bars. {map 6}

Porta al Prato

Narrow lanes give way to vast leafy paths here, where Le Cascine – the city's biggest park – draws those in need of a relaxing picnic or invigorating run. {map 6}

Porta Romana

Artisan jewellers, butchers and bookbinders have existed for generations on Porta Romana's quiet narrow streets, lending it a timeless air. Things are getting more modern, though, with contemporary art galleries, live music venues and local breweries drawing younger locals this way south. {map 3}

San Frediano

It's safe to say long-timers aren't best pleased with the gentrification of this sought-after Oltrarno area, but traditions are still going strong amid the new openings. Dusty artisan workshops thrive beside gourmet restaurants, and lively cocktail bars sit in the shadow of frescoed churches. {map 3}

San Lorenzo

Once a run-down district, San Lorenzo in the north has fast become one of the most popular areas to pass the day in, roaming Mercato Centrale, eating in affordable restaurants and clinking glasses in wine bars. {map 4}

San Marco

Home to the Accademia, San Marco is where visitors admire Michelangelo's *David*. Locals only pass through for the transport

links or, if they're students at the nearby uni, to mingle on the piazza. {map 4}

San Niccolò

With winding streets backing onto Florence's medieval walls, this small but picturesque Oltrarno district is like a village within the city. What it lacks in iconic monuments it makes up for in beautiful gardens, art studios, trendy *aperitivo* spots and a neighbourly community spirit. {map 5}

Sant'Ambrogio

Despite its central location, Sant'Ambrogio manages to remain off the main tourist path (and pretty calm). It's been home to a strong Jewish community for centuries, with the only kosher deli in the city and a huge synagogue. {map 2}

Santa Croce

Long-standing leather stores and the renowned Scuola del Cuoio hark back to a medieval Santa Croce, when it was a primary centre for tanners. Today, the area east of the centre is

just as important for the city's LGBTQ+ crowd, with its friendly venues and lively nightlife scene – one of the best in the city. {map 2}

Santa Maria Novella

Elegance defines this western area, its streets lined with perfumeries, high-end brands and fancy hotel bars. Yet it's not just about window-shopping down luxurious Via de' Tornabuoni. Locals do actually work in the area's many offices and studios, and take advantage of the great bars and restaurants on lunch breaks. {map 4}

Santo Spirito

When the Medici moved to the Palazzo Pitti in the 16th century, Santo Spirito went from being the city's poorest neighbourhood to one on everyone's radar. Despite its popularity, it's managed to retain an edge: a bohemian spirit infiltrates every art studio, quaint shop and cool bar, loved by the students and artists who proudly call the area home. {map 3}

Florence

ON THE MAP

Whether you're looking for your new favourite spot or want to check out what each part of Florence has to offer, our maps – along with handy map references throughout the book – have you covered.

ZAMBRA

A11

PERETOLA

Arn

ISOLOTTO

A1

CASELLINA

Greve

SCANDICCI

A1

0 kilometres   1

0 miles   1

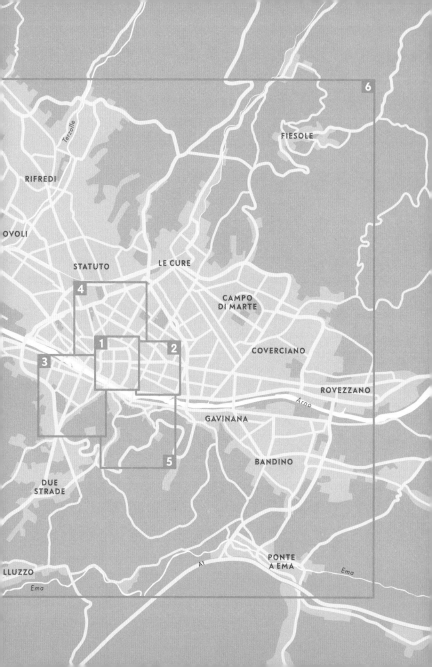

MAP 1

1

Vineria Sonora **D**

Pottery at Bottega Pendolare **A**

Jazz Club Firenze **N**

Teatro della Pergola **A**

La Sinagoga del Firenze **A**

Crisco Club **N**

Sbigoli Terrecotte **S**

FLY – Fashion Loves You Store **S**

Oblate Library **O**

Buca10 **N**

Piazza Sant'Ambrogio **N**

SANT' AMBROGIO

Pasticceria Nencioni **E**

Enoteca Alla Sosta dei Pa... **D**

Nove7 **N**

BORGO DEGLI ALBIZI

I Ghibellini **E**

La Gazza Ladra Gioielli **S**

John Borno **D**

Piazza dei Ciompi **O**

Tripperia Pollini Lampredotto **E**

Semel Street Food **E**

Locale **D**

Cibrèo Trattoria **E**

Fo'caccia la Notte **N**

Jewellery making at Linfa Studio Gallery **A**

Norcineria e Vineria della C.BIO **D**

Caffè Barni di Baracani Paolo **D**

PIAZZA LORENZO GHIBERTI **S** **E**

Teatro Verdi **A**

Bacco Nudo **D** **E**

Mercato di Sant'Ambrogio

SANTA CROCE

Malborghetto Pizzeria

A Ritroso A Rebour

Piazza Santa Croce **O**

Finisterrae **E**

Queer **N**

Soul Kitchen **N**

Basilica di Santa Croce **A**

Leather-making workshop **A**

Aquaflor **S**

Scuola del Cuoio **S**

Melaleuca **E**

MAP 2

Arno

Ponte A. Vespucci

SANTA MARIA NOVELLA

BORGO OGNISSANTI

LUNGARNO DEGLI ACCIAIOLO

V. DELLA VI...

PIAZZA CARLO GOLDONI

LUNGARNO CO...

Ponte alla Carraia

LUNGARNO GUICCIARD...

VIA DI SANTO SPIRITO

LUNGARNO

PIAZZA DI CESTELLO

SODERINI

VIA SANT' ONOFRIO

Trattoria Sabatino **E**

BORGO

SAN

FREDIANO

PIAZZA DE' NERLI

SAN FREDIANO

SAN FREDIANO

Mad Souls & Spirits **D**

Il Santo Bevitore **E** **S**

Heart to Heart in Florence **S**

Il Guscio **E**

Sagliano Concetti Sartorial **S**

Tabacchi Nuvola **N** **N**

NOF

Angela Caputi **D**

Gosh* **D**

Burro e Acciughe **E**

VIA DELL'ORTO

l'Brindellone **E**

Buonamici Bottega **S**

Pasticceria Buonamici

Piazza del Carmine **O**

Recollection di Albrici **S**

SANTO SPIRITO

Grimaldo Firenze **●**

VIALE ALEARDO ALEARDI

Cappella Brancacci **A**

VIA DEL LEONE

VIA SANTA MONACA

S. Forno **E** **E**

St Mark's English Church **A**

Circolo Aurora Firenze **N**

Piazza Tasso **O**

Sbrino Gelatificio Contadino

Santo Falafel **E**

VIA SANT' AGOSTINO

Alla Vecchia Bettola **E**

La Sorbettiera **E**

VIA DELLA CHIESA

VIA DEI SERRAGLI

Pop **D**

Piazza Santo Spirito **N**

Rasputin **D**

VIA DEL CAMPUCCIO

Loggia Roof Bar **D**

VIA DEL VILLANI

Giardino Torrigiani

Nokike Atelier **S**

Dalla Lola **S** **E**

Frau Leman **S**

Il Santo Vino **D**

VIA MAZZETTA

PIAZ... DE' PI...

Ostello Tasso **N**

VIALE FRANCESCO PETRARCA

Le Arti Orafe **S**

VIA DEI SERRAGLI

BORGO TEGOLAIO

Il Conventino Caffé Letterario **N**

VIA DEL CASONE

VIA ROMANA

VIA ROMANA

O

Giardino di Boboli

Riccardo Barthel **S**

PIAZZALE DELLA PORTA ROMANA

VIALE NICCOLÒ MACHIAVELLI

Pasticceria Gualtieri **E**

0 metres 250
0 yards 250

MAP 3

3

PIAZZA
DI SANTA
TRINITÀ

Ponte
Trinita

Arno

toria
nmillo

BORGO SAN JACOPO

jørk

Bulli e
N Ballene

VIA DEI GUICCIARDINI

D SDRONE

Pitti Gola e Cantina

Palazzo
Pitti

0 metres 250
0 yards 250

Fortezza
da Basso

Giardino della
Fortezza

VIALE F. STROZZI

VIALE SPARTACO
LAVAGNINI

VIA B. LUPI

VIA S. CATERINA D'ALESSANDRIA

Tiche Clothing Il Vegeteriar

VIALE FILIPPO STROZZI

Villa Vittoria

PIAZZA
DELL'
INDIPENDENZA

L'Olandese Volante

VIA XXVII APRILE

SRISA
Gallery

VIA GUELFA

VIA SAN GALLO

PIA
DI
MA

VIA FAENZA

Mostodolce

PIAZZA
ADUA

NAZIONALE

Vecchio
Forno

VIA

SimBIOsi
Coffee

GUELFA

Shake C

Stazione
Santa Maria
Novella

Sogni in Carta VIA

PIAZZA DEL
MERCATO
CENTRALE

Galle
dell'Accader

Melrose
Vintage Store

Da Nerbone

VIA C.

Casa del Vino

La Ménagère

Pasticceria
Deanna

PIAZZA
DELLA
STAZIONE

SAN
LORENZO

Cinema la
Compagnia

CAVOUR

PIAZZA DELL'
UNITÀ ITALIANA

PIAZZA DI SAN
LORENZO

VIA DEI CONTI

VIA DEI PUCCI

VIA DEI

Officina Profumo-Farmaceutica
di Santa Maria Novella

VIA DELLA SCALA

Street Levels
Gallery

Bar Galli

PIAZZA
DI SANTA
MARIA
NOVELLA

Arts Inn

Vini e Delizie

VIA DEI CERRETANI

PIAZZA SAN
GIOVANNI

PIAZZA DEL
DUOMO

VIA DEL PROCONSOLO

PALAZZUOLO

Museo Novecento

SANTA
MARIA
NOVELLA

BORGO OGNISSANTI

A Casa Ca.Fe

EFG Guanti

La Bottega della Frutta

Trattoria Marione

PIAZZA SAN
GIOVANNI

Tartan
Vintage

ottod'Ame

Farmacia
Münstermann

Mercatino dei Ninni

VIA DEI CALZAIUOLI

PIAZZA
DELLA
REPUBBLICA

VIA DEL CORSO

Benheart

VIA DE' TORNABUONI

DUOMO

Eduardo Secci Firenze

Paper marbling
with Riccardo Luci

Arno

MAP 4

PIAZZA
DELLA
LIBERTÀ

Caffè Lietta **D**

4

A SAN GALLO

CAVOUR

La Serra M.K.
Textile Atelier

CAMILLO

*Giardino dei
Semplici*

SAN
MARCO

Piazza della
Santissima
Annunziata
D

obiglio
E   Museo
A degli
Innocenti

a Mescita

VIA D ALFANI

nacia
issima
unziata

ZZA DI
A MARIA
JOVA

RGO DEGLI ALBIZI

SANTA
CROCE

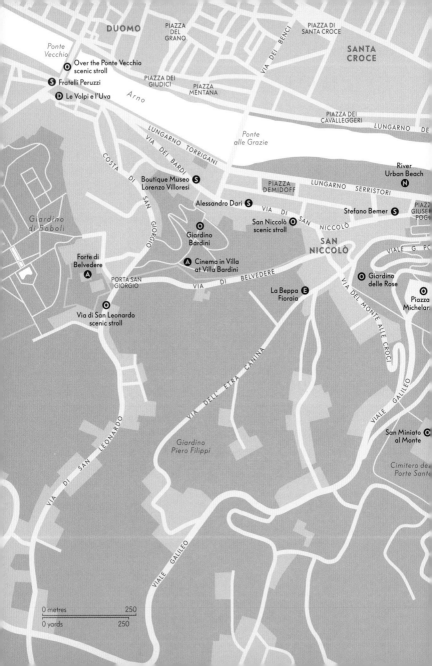

MAP 5

5

CA VECCHIA

Arno

N The Lodge

Giardino
dell'Iris
O

ALE MICHELANGIOLO

E EAT

La Beppa Fioraia *(p48)*

D DRINK

Le Volpi e l'Uva *(p73)*

S SHOP

Alessandro Dari *(p87)*

Boutique Museo Lorenzo Villoresi
(p91)

Fratelli Peruzzi *(p85)*

Stefano Bemer *(p92)*

A ARTS &
CULTURE

Cinema in Villa at Villa Bardini
(p125)

Forte di Belvedere *(p122)*

N NIGHTLIFE

The Lodge *(p150)*

River Urban Beach *(p140)*

O OUTDOORS

Giardino Bardini *(p172)*

Giardino dell'Iris *(p174)*

Giardino delle Rose *(p175)*

Over the Ponte Vecchio
scenic stroll *(p163)*

Piazzale Michelangelo *(p179)*

San Miniato al Monte *(p176)*

San Niccolò scenic stroll *(p161)*

Via di San Leonardo scenic
stroll *(p160)*

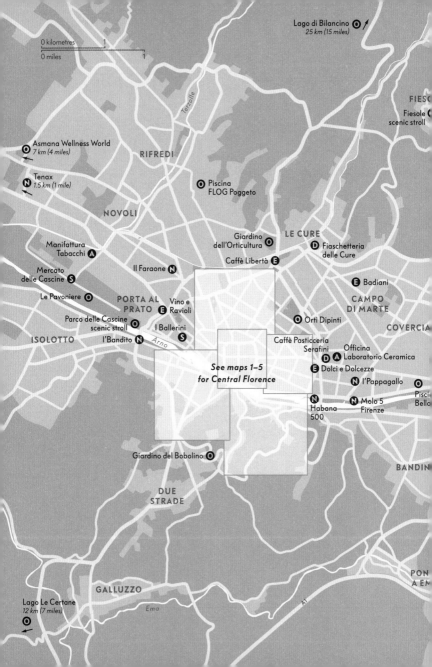

Lago di Bilancino ⊙ ↗
25 km (15 miles)

FIESO

Fiesole ◉
scenic stroll

Asmana Wellness World ⊙
7 km (4 miles)
←

Tenax Ⓝ
1.5 km (1 mile)
←

RIFREDI

Piscina ⊙
FLOG Poggeto

NOVOLI

LE CURE

Giardino ⊙
dell'Orticultura

Ⓓ Fiaschetteria
delle Cure

Caffè Libertà Ⓔ

Ⓔ Badiani

Manifattura Ⓐ
Tabacchi

Il Faraone Ⓝ

CAMPO
DI MARTE

Mercato Ⓢ
delle Cascine

Le Pavoniere ⊙

PORTA AL
PRATO

Vino e Ⓔ
Ravioli

COVERCIA

Parco delle Cascine
scenic stroll ⊙

I Ballerini Ⓢ

Orti Dipinti ⊙

Arno

Caffè Posticceria
Serafini

ISOLOTTO

l'Bandito Ⓝ

Ⓓ Officina Ⓐ
Laboratorio Ceramica

Ⓔ Dolci e Dolcezze

See maps 1–5
for Central Florence

Ⓝ l'Pappagallo

⊙ Pisci
Bello

Ⓝ
Habana
500

Ⓝ Molo 5
Firenze

Giardino del Bobolino ⊙

BANDIN

DUE
STRADE

GALLUZZO

Ema

PON
A EM

Lago Le Certane ⊙
12 km (7 miles)
←

AT

MAP 6

6

ROVEZZANO
Blanco
Beach Bar
InStabile –
Culture in Movimento

Ema

EAT

Tradition infiltrates every area of Florence's food scene. Mealtimes – a short breakfast, a long dinner – are sacred and the best recipes are always those nonna passed down.

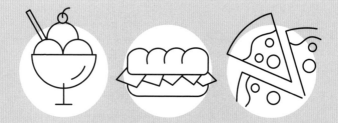

Breakfast Spots

*Forget everything you know about never-ending Italian meals. When it comes to breakfast, locals traditionally grab a **cornetto** (croissant) and a coffee, enjoyed standing at the bar of their local bakery.*

PASTICCERIA GUALTIERI

Map 3; Via Senese 18r, Porta Romana; ///speared.goat.renew; www.pasticceriagualtieri.com

The beauty of this bakery is its dedication to both time-honoured recipes and modern tastes. Bakers work the rolling pin daily, crafting *crostate di marmellata* (traditional jam tarts enjoyed at breakfast time) alongside the likes of vegan doughnuts and gluten-free puff pastries. It's totally acceptable to tuck into the flourless Iris Cake – made from a secret family recipe – for breakfast, by the way.

VECCHIO FORNO

Map 4; Via Guelfa 32, San Marco; ///deck.lasted.tuxedos; www.vecchiofornofirenze.it

If you find yourself fighting against the sweet tooth mentality that drives Florentines' breakfast choices, this little bakery will convert you. The piles of pastries are enough to make you go weak at the knees and

There are a couple of bar stools inside, but enjoy your treat as you walk to Galleria dell'Accademia around the corner.

resist all modes of decorum, powdered sugar falling upon you with every croissant bite. The pear and chocolate *torta* special is divine, as is the grape focaccia, made in the September harvest season.

A CASA CA.FE

Map 4; Via della Spada 47r, Santa Maria Novella;
///soda.charging.garages; www.acasacafe.it

A quick breakfast at the counter might be the Italian way, but many locals still cherish the pleasure of sitting down with a pastry and chatting over tiny cups of coffee. For those not rushing to work, the At Home Café is where to find solace before a day of meetings. Make yourself at home in a cosy corner, a cappuccino in one hand and a vegan brioche in the other.

I GHIBELLINI

Map 2; Piazza di San Pier Maggiore 8r, Sant'Ambrogio;
///tops.fizzled.tuned; www.ighibellini.com

Mornings always start the same way for Sant'Ambrogio's long-time residents, who stroll to this small spot after exchanging neighbourly pleasantries on the piazza. Manager Ambro seems to have their order memorized, an espresso and *bombolone* (light and tiny custard-filled doughnut) waiting on the counter as they approach the door.

» Don't leave without savouring a *cremino* – a traditional Florentine pastry filled with custard of just the right sweetness.

SHAKE CAFÉ

Map 4; Via Camillo Cavour 69r, San Marco;
///goodbye.stud.wooden; www.shakecafe.bio

Florence might cling relentlessly to its traditions (speedy breakfasts being a prime example), but young Florentines have learned to love the city's burgeoning brunch scene. Truth be told, brunch mirrors the joy of Italian meals: lingering at the table, enjoying good conversation and feasting on great food. These are the exact scenes you'll find at Shake on the weekend, when effortlessly chic Italians gossip over a chai latte and cheese and kimchi toasties.

ROBIGLIO

Map 4; Via dei Servi 112r, San Marco; ///secrets.dream.busters;
www.robiglio1928.it

Florence's speedy *al bar* experience can be intimidating at the best of times, let alone during the morning rush hour, when noisy coffee machines amp up your heart rate before the caffeine even kicks in. Speed is still of the essence at this family-run café, but the refined air

Shh!

Keep an eye out at Coffee Mantra: this Sant'Ambrogio spot often hosts Wild Buns Bakery (*www.wildbunsbakery. com*), a Scandinavian pop-up.

It was opened by Robert, who left his job in Estonia and moved to Florence to follow his passion for baking. Try his cinnamon buns – they're divine.

invokes a sense of calm. Loyal customers have been propping up the elegant marble counter since 1928, chatting with the bartender between bites of a *scendiletto* (a pastry filled with custard and lemon), before swiftly moving on when the last crumb has been devoured.

FINISTERRAE

Map 2; Piazza Santa Croce 12, Santa Croce; ///villas.shampoo.chill;
www.finisterraefirenze.com

Students from Santa Croce's many language schools always convene at Finisterrae after early classes, indulging in a mid-morning breakfast on the sunny piazza. The cute pastries, paired with the city's best soy milk cappuccinos, are the perfect bite-size sugar hit before the next class starts.

MELALEUCA

Map 2; Lungarno delle Grazie 18, Santa Croce; ///loafer.molars.lost;
055 614 6892

Yes, the international brunch scene has managed to make big inroads in Florence. But this gorgeous Aussie café doesn't overlook the city it calls home. Owners Chloe and Marco ensure that everything – the almond milk, home-cured bacon, vanilla essence – is made on-site, lending a Florentine touch to the quality. Little wonder it's such a hit with both Italians and expats, who enjoy bagels and eggs on the tiny pavement tables from 10am.

» Don't leave without taking a cinnamon bun away. Served soft and warm from the oven, they're the best Scandi bakes this side of Denmark.

Lunch Spots

Scoffing lunch at your desk is virtually unheard of in Florence, where there's always time to savour a leisurely meal in the sun or set up shop in a cosy café. Lunchtime is often when the best deals are, too.

CASELLA 18

Map 1; Via Santa Elisabetta 18, Duomo; ///interval.blessing.infuses; 055 285 595

When Italians are homesick for a big family meal, this restaurant is like a hug on a plate. The carb-heavy menu features everything you'd find at Sunday lunch in a Tuscan home: chicken liver pate *crostini*, cold-cuts, organic cheeses, tortelloni, pizza. You'll likely leave on a first-name basis with the staff, who forgive your bad Italian while they recommend dishes with an infectious smile and the odd joke.

BAR GALLI

Map 4; Via dei Banchi 14, Santa Maria Novella; ///reserve.shocked.silk

You can't help but speak lovingly of this bar, known locally as Dalla Piera in honour of the fabulous 70-something owner. Piera is the classic Italian mamma, spending the day preparing a *ciambellone* cake made using her great-great-grandma's secret recipe. When

As day turns into night, Bar Galli turns from traditional Italian bar to Banki Ramen, a beloved Japanese spot serving noodles.

the cake's out of the oven, she's often behind the counter with her son and niece, welcoming you in with the call of *amore bello* (beautiful love) before serving you a sandwich – and a slice of cake, of course.

S.FORNO

Map 3; Via Santa Monaca 3r, Santo Spirito; ///miracle.machine.evidence; www.ilsantobevitore.com

S.Forno isn't well signposted, but the scent of warm bread and the hushed chatter of mothers queuing for sourdough loaves insist you're in the right place. This century-old bakery is one of the few to still bake its bread on-site, the ovens fired up at the crack of dawn to meet the lunchtime made-to-order panini rush. Enjoy yours at a little table, watching shoppers drift in and out with baguettes under their arms.

I'BRINDELLONE

Map 3; Piazza Piattelina 10, San Frediano; ///pens.similar.will; 055 217 879

Slick service and even basic manners – especially towards tourists – are lacking at this workers' café, but the great value makes the odd grunt at your inability to speak Italian worth it. Sit beside grocers and construction workers for a two-course lunch (pasta followed by meat or fish) with a quarter carafe of house wine for just €11.

» Don't leave without ordering a dessert of *cantucci biscotti*, a Tuscan staple dating back to pre-Roman times.

Solo, Pair, Crowd

The beauty of a carb-loving city is the seemingly endless spots that dish up pizza, be it by the slice to indulge in alone or a cheesy feast for two.

FLYING SOLO

A slice of the action

Pick a slice from the display at La Divina Pizza in Sant'Ambrogio and thank the foodie gods that you won't have to offer anyone a bite of your sourdough treat.

IN A PAIR

Not so cheesy date

You're in Florence, so you needn't wait for the evening to date. Book a table in the upstairs area at Sophia Loren – a stylish pizzeria in Santa Maria Novella, inspired by the Italian diva's origins – and make eyes over a margherita.

FOR A CROWD

Pizza party

Starita a Materdei in San Marco is the quintessential Neapolitan pizzeria – so good, you'll want to try everything on the menu. Order a few options and get sharing.

IL VEGETARIANO

Map 4; Via delle Ruote 30r, San Marco; ///brighter.toasted.required;
www.il-vegetariano.com

While vegetarian cuisine isn't difficult to come by in Florence, it tends to play second fiddle to T-bone steaks. Not so at Il Vegetariano, which has been championing veggie food and appeasing meat-free eaters since 1981. Tuck into wholesome dishes like porcini and white bean soup on communal tables, no raw steaks dangling from above.

MALBORGHETTO PIZZERIA

Map 2; Via dei Macci 76r, Sant'Ambrogio; ///roadmap.regard.poems;
www.malborghettofirenze.it

Pizza might hail from Naples, but it's loved just as much in Florence. Malborghetto is the place to go for proper Neapolitan pizza, made using slow-rise dough and devoured by friends at a huge table.
» Don't leave without topping your pizza with top-quality *fior di latte* mozzarella or Tuscan sausage, for an additional charge.

DALLA LOLA

Map 3; Via della Chiesa 16r, Santo Spirito; ///destined.cricket.soldiers;
055 265 4354

Chef Matilde Pettini is shaking up the notion that *osteries* are afraid to change. With her modernization of the time-honoured restaurant that formerly stood here, she's convinced a young crowd to go wild for traditional dishes like chicken hearts and offal by giving them a new twist. The natural wine pairings help matters, too.

Street Food

For every elegant bistro or rustic trattoria there's a time-honoured kiosk or beloved market stall offering up a **merenda** *(mid-afternoon snack). Tuck in while strolling the streets or settle on a piazza.*

DA NERBONE

Map 4; Mercato Centrale, San Lorenzo; ///liver.veto.theme; 339 648 0251

You'll need to channel a no-nonsense mentality to get to Nerbone, which is tucked inside the bustling Mercato Centrale. This blue-collar canteen on the ground floor has been feeding hungry market traders since 1872 with *trippa alla fiorentina* (tripe and tomato stew) and pasta *al ragù*. Grab a tray and eat your chosen dish at the bar counter while practising your Italian with the regulars.

I DUE FRATELLINI

Map 1; Via dei Cimatori 38r, Duomo; ///bars.jolly.starter; 055 239 6096

The infamous All'Antico Vinaio is the Uffizi of sandwich shops in Florence: every tourist wants in on its world-famous food, and will queue for an hour to make it happen. Not so the locals, who glide past these crowds on their lunch breaks, whistling while they walk to I Due Fratellini instead, a hole-in-the-wall joint where high-quality paninis have been made in mere minutes since 1875. Choose between 30 different fillings, from the likes of pecorino cheese from Siena to goat's cheese from Maremma, before smugly tucking in on the nearby piazza.

» **Don't leave without** ordering a glass of wine. The wine cellar is well stocked, and there's usually a bottle of something already open.

TRIPPERIA POLLINI LAMPREDOTTO
Map 2; Via dei Macci 126, Sant'Ambrogio; ///spilled.leaflet.tougher; www.tripperiapollini.com

Lampredotto – a historic Florentine staple made from the fourth stomach of the cow – isn't for the faint-hearted. But to say you've tried it is to gain a badge of honour. Everyone has their go-to stall, and for ravenous local workers and students, it's this van. White-aproned chefs serve up a healthy dose of the latest neighbourhood gossip while they stuff *lampredotto,* stewed in tomato sauce, into a pillowy bread bun. The slowly cooked meat is not a hundred miles from a Sloppy Joe, so pick up extra napkins and find a bench.

Shh!

Given its lesser-trodden location on Piazza Nerli in San Frediano, La Buticche di Lampredotto doesn't get the same traffic as most *lampredotto* stalls. It's just as good as any, though, and owner Simone is always chatty while he prepares your meaty sandwich.

VINO E RAVIOLI

Map 6; Via del Ponte alle Mosse 7r, Porta al Prato;
///keep.massing.future; 348 330 6334

"Wine and Ravioli" might sound like your archetypal Italian joint, but the name of this relaxed spot masks its most prized offerings: Chinese street food staples. For just €5, you can get six dumplings and a glass of red or white wine. The staff might even teach you some Mandarin words while they prepare your order.

» Don't leave without trying the delectable Chinese omelette, deep-fried and filled with ham and cheese.

I'TOSTO

Map 1; Via dei Servi 8r, Duomo; ///clever.fines.sprawls; 055 010 8870

It's a classic story: you've spent hours gazing at the noble Duomo when, suddenly, your rumbling stomach has passersby stopping in their tracks. Keep those concerned glances at bay with a super-sized sandwich from I'Tosto. This little spot is hidden down a side street facing the Duomo, so you can still worship Brunelleschi's masterpiece while crumbs collect on your coat.

MERCATO DI SANT'AMBROGIO

Map 2; Piazza Lorenzo Ghiberti, Sant'Ambrogio;
///singing.glaze.grandson; www.mercatosantambrogio.it

Quality, seasonal ingredients are the greatest joy of Italian food, and picking them up from this market is part of that pleasure (even if it means the odd shove from a local if you dawdle too long). Grab the

The nearby Murate Art District has many benches where you can sit down to eat and relax if Piazza Ciompi is brimming.

attention of a vendor reading the paper and pick up whatever's in season – peaches and freshly churned ricotta; bread, olives and sundried tomatoes – to assemble a DIY picnic in Piazza Ciompi.

SANTO FALAFEL

Map 3; Via Sant'Agostino 28r, Santo Spirito; ///kilts.escapes.beeline; 347 874 0278

Florentines might be known for their love of hearty, carb-heavy feasts, but they're equally fond of light, healthy dishes. Doling out vegan Middle Eastern food, this popular spot on the Oltrarno never leaves you in a post-lunch slump. It's a big hit with Santo Spirito's tribe of creatives, who order takeaway boxes of tabbouleh, vine-leaf sarma and baba ganoush to fuel them for the afternoon.

SEMEL STREET FOOD

Map 2; Piazza Lorenzo Ghiberti 44r, Sant'Ambrogio; ///civic.pixies.lucky

When owner Marco tells you they're out of everything at 1:30pm, he's not joking. Perched by the entrance to Mercato di Sant'Ambrogio, this thimble-sized sandwich shop feeds exhausted shoppers who've just picked up their dinner supplies. Marco welcomes them with a calming smile, a glass of red and one type of sandwich: small, round *semelino* panini with unusual fillings like truffle with pear or anchovies with orange. Arrive early or miss out.

Traditionally Tuscan

Tuscans have been cooking simple, seasonal dishes – robust bean stews, tender pork roasts, thick minestrone soups – for centuries. Age-old recipes served in rustic spots are still the pride of Florentines.

TRATTORIA MARIONE

Map 4; Via della Spada 27r, Santa Maria Novella;
///quietly.unwanted.scuba; www.trattoriamarione.it

Imagine the archetypal trattoria – wood panelling, gold lettering, bunches of garlic in the window – and you've got Marione. Inside, patterned crockery is placed on checkered tablecloths and old boys sit elbow to elbow, passing red wine around the table while hollering over one another. The thick *ribollita* (bread soup) and rich wild boar pasta complete this quintessential picture.

CIBRÈO TRATTORIA

Map 2; Via dei Macci 122r, Sant'Ambrogio; ///arrived.blizzard.flow;
www.cibreo.com

For many Florentines, their most cherished moments were spent in nonna's kitchen, watching her whip up the best meals in a messy apron. If it's the new generation's responsibility to preserve Italian family recipes, then late Cibrèo owner Fabio Picci has done his nonna proud with the legacy he's left behind. Cibrèo's menu pays homage to the wonderful flavours that defined Fabio's childhood, from the namesake cibrèo (chicken offal) stew his mamma used to cook to the off-menu chicken head that's frankly not for the squeamish.

ALLA VECCHIA BETTOLA
Map 3; Viale Vasco Pratolini 3/5/7, San Frediano;
///dinosaur.funnels.vaccines; 055 224 158

You know you're in a restaurant that doesn't take tradition seriously if they agree to serve *bistecca alla fiorentina* (Florentine steak) well done. Old-fashioned Alla Vecchia Bettola would never stand for such sacrilege; here, it's served rare under the watchful eye of hanging cured meats, or not at all. While it's tempting to polish off the bottle of house wine you'll wash it down with, leaving a few drops behind is the classier move, and might earn you a complimentary *digestivo*.

» Don't leave without ordering the fiery *penne alla bettola* (pasta in vodka sauce), which will have you entirely rethinking tomato sauce.

Try it!
COOK LIKE A TUSCAN

Tuscan cooking is centred on the passing down of knowledge, and MaMa Florence cooking school (*www.mamaflorence.com*) does just that. Learn how to cook Tuscan meat or select the best veggies here.

TRATTORIA SABATINO

Map 3; Via Pisana 2r, San Frediano; ///examine.calculating.zipped;
www.trattoriasabatino.it

Nothing brings Italian families together like the dinner table, and
family-run Sabatino has given Italians a table to turn to since 1956.
Written up daily on a typewriter, the menu is a mix of simple
standbys like *panzanella* (Italian bread and tomato salad) and
rotating specials. Expect to be seated at a communal table, where
generations of regulars welcome you like a warm embrace.

VINI E VECCHI SAPORI

Map 1; Via dei Magazzini 3r, Duomo; ///lonely.ally.hounded;
055 0293 045

"No pizza, no ice, no take-away, no spritz, no cappuccino" reads the
old-school menu at this rustic little warren. Instead, ask for a hearty dish
that allows Tuscany's flavoursome ingredients to shine, like *bistecca*
or *paccheri* (big pasta) – you might even raise a smile from the owner.

LA MESCITA

Map 4; Via degli Alfani 70r, San Marco; ///retiring.online.tulip;
347 7951 604

La Mescita feels like coming home. The staff greet you warmly at
the door, the ceiling fans whirr above nonni playing cards and the
divine smell of pasta with wild boar *ragù* permeates the tiny room.
» Don't leave without trying the *crostini ai fegatini*: a signature
appetizer prepared with chicken liver pate, butter and crusty bread.

Liked by the locals

"When I'm craving something delicious and simple – the kind of food I'd cook at home – I always choose a trattoria. My favourite? Sabatino, where you can feel the friendly atmosphere as soon as you walk through the door."

FRANCESCO MANNARINO, LEATHER GOODS TECHNICIAN AT PRADA AND SOMMELIER

Leisurely Dinners

A long, relaxed dinner is the Florentine way, where courses are never rushed, bottles of wine are poured between guests and good conversation is as important as what's on your plate.

LA BEPPA FIORAIA
Map 5; Via dell'Erta Cantina 6r, San Niccolò;
///mammal.declining.clothed; www.beppafioraia.it

As the Italian saying goes, *a tavola non s'invecchia* ("at the table, one does not grow old"). Those who settle on the long tables at this serene garden restaurant are indeed oblivious to the passing of time, their phones tucked away as they lose an evening in the flower-perfumed summer air. Laughter deepens with every carafe of Chianti passed between friends, and every forkful of pasta.

IL GUSCIO
Map 3; Via dell'Orto 49, San Frediano; ///surely.domestic.graphic;
www.ristorante-ilguscio.it

This upmarket trattoria serves up generous portions to San Frediano locals, who keep Il Guscio deservedly busy. Fish-heavy dishes fly out of the kitchen, satisfying hungry patrons whose cacophonous voices

If you're on a budget, go at lunchtime for a more casual and cheaper version of the dinnertime service.

bellow out for organic wine. Follow those who've been coming here since the 1980s and order one of their old favourites: the tuna tartare or fillet steak.

RISTORANTE NUGOLO

Map 2; Via della Mattonaia 27r, Sant'Ambrogio; ///started.margin.drive; www.ilnugolo.com

If Tuscany is Italy's orchard and vegetable garden, Nugolo is Florence's. Here, fine ingredients are cultivated in an allotment and used for ultra-seasonal reimaginings of 19th-century recipes. Watch on longingly as chefs prepare your supper in a glass-fronted open kitchen, designed to look like a greenhouse.

>> **Don't leave without** ordering a dish with tomatoes. Nugolo is named after a heritage tomato, one of 200 grown in the owner's allotment.

BURRO E ACCIUGHE

Map 3; Via dell'Orto 35, San Frediano; ///infinite.chill.reclaim; www.burroeacciughe.com

Seafood that's worth writing home about can be tough to find in a non-coastal city, but Burro e Acciughe might just tempt you to buy a postcard. The menu feels finely curated rather than overstuffed with everything under the sea, and the manageable portions won't leave you in a post-dinner slump. Order fried anchovies for your appetizer, tagliatelle with baby squid as a first dish and tuna steak as your second, asking the staff for the best wine pairings as you go.

Liked by the locals

"More than a meal, Italy's *cenetta tranquilla* is a state of mind: you sit at the table, you chit-chat, you take a bite, sip a glass of wine and let the evening go. No watches needed."

VINCENZO D'ANGELO, DIGITAL PROJECT MANAGER AND WRITER

IL SANTO BEVITORE

Map 3; Via di Santo Spirito 64, Santo Spirito; ///engine.indicate.lame; www.ilsantobevitore.com

If anywhere encapsulates the Italian art of *cenetta tranquilla* – a long, heart-warming dinner with loved ones – it's Il Santo Bevitore. Run by three childhood friends, this bustling spot is where catch-ups happen over candlelight. Guests go all out on the *primi* (first courses) and *secondi* (second courses), lingering over the seasonal dishes as they swap stories and get their wine topped up by stylish staff. By the time *dolci* (dessert) is served with a glass of bitter *amaro*, the cobblestones outside will be springing to life with people starting their nights out.

» **Don't leave without** ordering the daily special. It could be duck leg with chicory, pappardelle pasta with wild boar or anything in between.

TRATTORIA CAMMILLO

Map 3; Borgo San Jacopo 57r, Santo Spirito; ///powers.internal.demoted; 055 212 427

When large Florentine families meet for a meal outside of mamma's home, it's this trattoria that they turn to. Though any and every Italian will vouch that no one cooks a better dinner than the women in their family, Cammillo is the master of home-style Italian cooking, and has made a name for itself by outdoing nonnas at their own recipes since 1945. Raucous family feasts ensue here on the weekend, when siblings swap news between slurps of vegetarian *ribollita* soup and nonni tuck into towering scoops of persimmon tiramisu. This isn't a place for the carb-fearful, nor those who expect white tablecloths to still be white at the end of a meal.

Sweet Treats

With bakeries and gelateria *seemingly on every corner, the awakening whiff of a sugary snack is never far away. Florentines wear the "birthplace of* gelato*" badge with pride, indulging in it no matter the hour.*

DOLCI E DOLCEZZE

Map 6; Piazza Cesare Beccaria 8r, Sant'Ambrogio; ///hounded.tribune.rocked; 055 234 5458

Well-heeled Florentines often pop into this dainty turquoise *pasticceria* (bakery) before a dinner party, selecting a handful of miniature pastries to spoil their host with. The perfectly formed tartlets, cased in delicate shortbread, change with the seasons – wild strawberry in summer, crème brûlée in winter – and are beautifully displayed under the glint of glass chandeliers.

SBRINO GELATIFICIO CONTADINO

Map 3; Via dei Serragli 32r, Santo Spirito; ///clerics.makes.notebook; 055 012 2286

Florentines know that the way to tell a good *gelateria* is by how creamy, soft and fresh the *gelato* is. It's safe to say they've spent enough time tucking into the dessert to label Sbrino as one of the best, given the vegan options, seasonal flavours and natural ingredients used. Of the three branches across the city, the Santo Spirito outpost is the go-to on the weekends, when it's open until midnight and serves party-goers cult favourite flavours like zabaglione or *speculoos* cookie.

» Don't leave without asking the staff which flavours to pair. Dark chocolate sorbet with lemon and mint is an unlikely winner.

PASTICCERIA BUONAMICI
Map 3; Via dell'Orto 27r, San Frediano; ///investor.start.softest; 055 224 004

This *pasticceria* is committed to keeping traditions alive. The first chefs start at 3:30am, firing up the ovens just as they've done since the bakery was founded in 1949. By 7am, the counter gleams with time-honoured treats like *cantucci* or, on Sundays only, *la fedora* – a Florentine chocolate cake that most bakeries have long forgotten. While second-generation owner Roberto is still involved in the proceedings, it's his daughter Rossella who's mostly on the shop floor these days, debating the latest social issues with the regulars.

Try it!
BAKE A CAKE

While you're at Pasticceria Buonamici, book a hands-on cooking class with head pastry chef Francesco. He'll share his passion for seasonal Tuscan bakes such as chestnut cake and almond-crusted *torta della nonna*.

CAFFÈ LIBERTÀ

Map 6; Piazza della Libertà, 27r, Campo di Marte;
///conquest.loving.mended; 055 474 978

The only thing more delightful than the Italian *al banco* (at the bar) tradition is the *pastarelle della Domenica* (Sunday pastries) ritual, and Caffè Libertà prizes both. After long, carb-filled lunches with friends, laissez-faire locals stroll towards this café for a sweet dessert. Order a pistachio cream-filled croissant – likely fresh out of the oven – and consume it at the counter with extra napkins.

PASTICCERIA NENCIONI

Map 2; Via Pietrapiana 24r, Sant'Ambrogio; ///remedy.transmit.drag;
055 241 012

As soon as the church bells ring out at 4pm, the time for a *merenda* (afternoon snack) officially begins. Giddy schoolchildren plead with their parents to take them to Nencioni, where a queue quickly forms to secure a *budino di riso* (rice pudding in a shortcrust case) fresh

What looks like your everyday backdoor at Via del Campo d'Arrigo 14r actually opens to l'Pastaio, a large pastry shop serving bars and *pasticcerie* across the city. It's open to the public every night from 10pm to 5am, selling delicious pastries at a steal – a *cornetto* will only set you back €1.

from the oven. Save the disappointment of them selling out and pop by in the morning instead, when a steady stream of regulars point out the mini puff pastries they'd like beautifully wrapped.

LA SORBETTIERA
Map 3; Piazza Tasso 11r, San Frediano; ///uniform.cocktail.soon; www.lasorbettiera.it

Antonio Ciabattoni was just 14 when he started working at a *gelato* shop in Germany, spending his teenage summers learning the tricks of the trade from the Brustolon family. All that knowledge has been poured into his own tiny shop, where he serves sardonic San Frediano residents *gelato*, made using a mix of classic and modern techniques. He's always ready with a smile and flavour suggestion, be it the Thai made with lemongrass or the salted caramel.

» Don't leave without topping your scoop(s) with a complimentary cookie to up that inevitable sugar high.

BADIANI
Map 6; Viale dei Mille 20r, Campo di Marte; ///luxury.fashion.awake; www.gelateriabadiani.it

A stone's throw from the Artemio Franchi Stadium, Badiani has fast become the spot for Fiorentina football fans to indulge post-victory or find sweet solace post-defeat. It even has its own mascot, if you will: the Buontalenti flavour, made of just cream, milk, sugar and eggs. Named after the 16th-century architect credited with inventing *gelato*, it's unique to Florence – at least that's something to celebrate.

An afternoon
indulging in gelato

Florence is the birthplace of *gelato* as we know it. Back in 1559, as most stories go, architect Bernardo Buontalenti was tasked with organizing a banquet at the Medici court. He invented a new dessert for the occasion, flavoured with citrus and chilled using his own ice storage system. The treat quickly spread across the city and beyond, and locals have been enjoying a small cup after work or dinner ever since. To enjoy gelato at its best, avoid the inauthentic colourful mounds in tourist hotspots and savour fresh flavours at these *gelaterie*.

1. ARÀ
Via Giosuè Carducci 55, Sant'Ambrogio; www.araesicilia.it
///door.advances.hotel

2. Vivoli
Via dell'Isola delle Stinche 7r, Santa Croce; www.vivoli.it
///resort.boxing.surreal

3. Perché no!...
Gelato Academy
Via dei Tavolini 19r, Duomo; 055 239 8969
///tribal.manages.river

4. La Carraia
Piazza Nazario Sauro 25r, San Frediano; 055 280 695
///device.stale.somebody

My Sugar ///dashes.staked.tabloid

Gelateria Edoardo ///sublime.fats.ensemble

**Get a sugar hit at
LA CARRAIA**
When you fancy a gelato fix but can't face a huge helping, this spot sells mini scoops for €1. Order a ricotta and pear and enjoy.

SANTO SPIRITO

PIAZZA DI SANTO SPIRITO

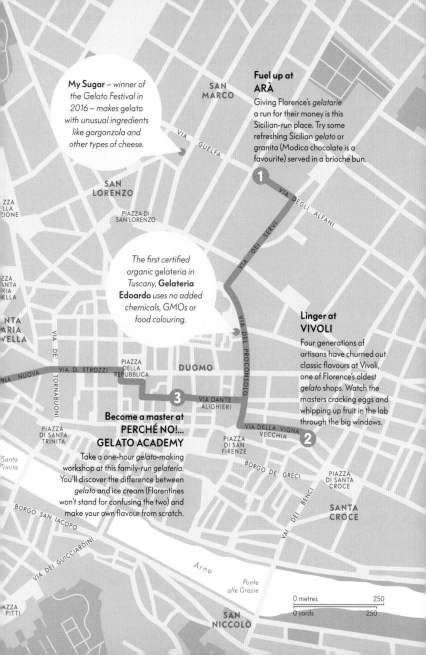

My Sugar – winner of the Gelato Festival in 2016 – makes gelato with unusual ingredients like gorgonzola and other types of cheese.

Fuel up at ARÀ

Giving Florence's *gelatarie* a run for their money is this Sicilian-run place. Try some refreshing Sicilian *gelato* or granita (Modica chocolate is a favourite) served in a brioche bun.

The first certified organic gelateria in Tuscany, **Gelateria Edoardo** uses no added chemicals, GMOs or food colouring.

Linger at VIVOLI

Four generations of artisans have churned out classic flavours at Vivoli, one of Florence's oldest *gelato* shops. Watch the masters cracking eggs and whipping up fruit in the lab through the big windows.

Become a master at PERCHÉ NO!... GELATO ACADEMY

Take a one-hour *gelato*-making workshop at this family-run *gelateria*. You'll discover the difference between *gelato* and ice cream (Florentines won't stand for confusing the two) and make your own flavour from scratch.

DRINK

An espresso before work, a glass of Chianti with lunch, a negroni while the sun sets – stopping for a sip of something delicious is a daily ritual to be indulged.

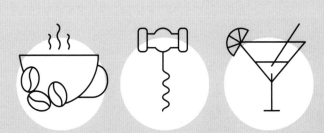

Historic Cafés

Long-standing cafés testify to the local love of whiling away the hours in an opulent setting. Very little beats the pleasure of sipping a drink in these historic spaces, many of which have inspired great minds.

SCUDIERI

Map 1; Piazza di San Giovanni 19r, Duomo; ///biggest.stop.sometime; www.scudieri.it

Things have little changed at this elegant café since it opened in 1939. The same chandeliers gleam from above, baristas still don a coat and tie, and espressos are forever gulped at the marble bar. Sophistication spills out onto the terrace, too, where friends cradle a cup of coffee while overlooking the Duomo.

CAFFÈ CONCERTO PAZKOWSKI

Map 1; Piazza della Repubblica 6, Duomo; ///briefer.wacky.lodge; www.caffepaszkowski.com

A brewery in the 1800s, Pazkowski made a real name for itself in the 20th century when it evolved into a caffè-concert hall. The all-female orchestra swiftly became a hallmark of Florentine evenings, not least for the Italian intellectuals who would debate politics while piano notes hung in the air. Though the crowd is less literary and more glitzy these days, mates and dates still gather here at night for a classic martini and a swing concert (artistic debates optional).

CAFFÈ LIETTA

Map 4; Piazza della Libertà 6-8r, San Marco; ///noses.belts.richly;
www.caffelietta.it

History isn't tied up in bricks and mortar here. Rather, founded by the granddaughters of fashion designer Roberto Cavalli, Lietta is the carrier of the negroni legacy. Roberto once owned the now-closed Caffè Giacosa, named after the original spot where, in the 1920s, Count Camillo Negroni sauntered in and requested a boozier version of the Milano-Torino. Despite the new location and name, Lietta still has traces of Giacosa, like the porcelain cups that coffees are served in, or the wrought iron chairs that fill up at *aperitivo* hours.

CAFFÈ RIVOIRE

Map 1; Piazza della Signoria 5r, Duomo; ///voter.shields.homes;
www.rivoire.it

Though it's seen as a Florentine icon, Rivoire — and its style of chocolatiering — is tied to Turin, the home city of founder Enrico Rivoire. This café is where Florentines learned how to taste chocolate back in 1872, and they've been indulging in it ever since, popping by for a decadent hot chocolate to stave off the chills come winter.

» **Don't leave without** picking up a little red box of the famous CC hazelnut cream, produced by the chocolate factory on-site.

CAFFÈ GILLI

Map 1; Via Roma 1r, Duomo; ///briskly.storms.chin;
www.caffegilli.com

As Florence's oldest and most opulent café, Gilli is the best for bells and whistles with your drink: coffered ceilings, crystal chandeliers and caramel-marble tables. Since its founding by a Swiss family in 1733, and through its relocation in the early 1900s, Gilli has remained a fashionable meeting place to see and – most importantly – be seen. Soak up the timeless elegance in the gilded back room, where your table might have seated the great thinkers of the 1900s or famous fashion designers passing through for Pitti Uomo (p9).

>> **Don't leave without** staying for cocktail hour, when barman and negroni expert Luca Picchi serves up the classic drink.

GIUBBE ROSSE

Map 1; Piazza della Repubblica 13/14r, Duomo;
///sour.remotes.cats; 055 212 280

This café opened as Reininghaus in the late 19th century, but when locals struggled to pronounce the name, they referred to it as the bar "where they wear the red (rosse) jackets (giubbe)". The moniker caught on, and it wasn't long before its notoriety grew beyond the waitstaff's attire. Giubbe Rosse became a hub for the burgeoning Futurist art movement and magazine bodies holding meetings, these groups likely enticed by the lively vibe and global newspapers on display. This artistic heritage is alive and well today: long-timers in tailored suits leaf through newspapers and budding writers scribble on a napkins when the right amount of caffeine hits.

Liked by the locals

"Why is it that coffee in Italy tastes so delicious? It might have less to do with the actual beans or the way the milk is frothed, and more with the sociable ritual of drinking it. The joy of drinking coffee is deep rooted in our society."

ANNARITA TRANCHESE, ITALIAN TEACHER AT PAROLA

Coffee Bars

Italians take their coffee seriously. Whether it's a quick espresso at the counter of an old-world café or a cup nursed in a third-wave roastery, it's less about the caffeine hit and more about pleasure.

CAFFÈ DELL'ORO

Map 1; Lungarno degli Acciaiuoli 4, Duomo; ///haggle.briefer.subsets; www.lungarnocollection.com

Stationed between Florence's famous bridges – the Ponte Vecchio and Ponte Santa Trinita – this bouji pavement bar is arguably the city's best people-watching spot. As you savour a cappuccino and homemade biscotti on the luxe low tables, watching cyclists weave around besotted honeymooners, the lofty prices suddenly seem worthwhile.

CAFFÈ PASTICCERIA SERAFINI

Map 6; Via Vincenzo Gioberti 168r, Piazza Beccaria, Sant'Ambrogio; ///lectures.martini.requests; www.pasticceriaserafini.it

Coffee stood at the bar, bantering with the barista about the football or the weather, is a morning practice that Italians hold sacred. For the proper *al bar* experience without another English accent in earshot, hit up this local *pasticceria* and ask for a *fornacino* (in

Italy has a sweet tradition of *caffè sospeso* (suspended coffee): you pay in advance for a person who can't afford a cup.

Italian, *per favore*). This small cappuccino is a Serafini speciality, topped with powdered cacao and chopped dark chocolate that sinks to the bottom and melts. Enjoy it at the counter, naturally.

SIMBIOSI COFFEE

Map 4; Via Guelfa 64r, San Marco; ///bless.fever.outwit; www.simbiosi.bio

In a city where asking for a cappuccino after 12pm will more than likely result in an exasperated, eye-rolling barista, SimBIOsi is a safe haven. It's all down to its hip team, who not only tolerate but welcome requests for chai lattes, flat whites and other such sacrilege that traditional places won't stand for. The organic coffee used, sourced directly from Florentine start-up D612, is divine.

» Don't leave without ordering a *caffè latte d'avena con ghiaccio*, an iced oat milk latte that you won't find anywhere else in Florence.

CAFFE BARNI DI BARACANI PAOLO

Map 2; Mercato di Sant'Ambrogio, Piazza Lorenzo Ghiberti, Sant'Ambrogio; ///charging.sneezed.raking; 055 248 0778

Nowhere fuels morning grocery shops quite like this no-nonsense café inside Sant'Ambrogio market. It's run by a handful of friendly but chaotic women, yelling orders at one another as they serve strong coffees. Down your drink at the bar and move on – this isn't somewhere to linger, and definitely isn't somewhere to fuss around ordering anything other than an espresso or cappuccino.

Solo, Pair, Crowd

The Italian coffee break is a moment to be savoured. Nurse a cup alone or enjoy with friends.

FLYING SOLO
While away the day
Spend an undisturbed afternoon reading or studying at La Cité, an offbeat spot in San Frediano filled with books. Before you know it, your coffee cup will be switched out for a beer bottle (it drifts into a bar at night).

IN A PAIR
Tea for two
Days in Florence don't truly start until you've had caffeine, but it needn't come in the form of coffee. When your mum's in town, take her to the darling Santo Spirito outpost of La Via del Tè and choose from 250 types of tea to pour. It's joyfully vintage.

FOR A CROWD
Coffee, cake and chats
Weekend catch-ups with the gang are best had at Budellino in Santa Croce, where big communal tables lie at the back. Order coffee with a cake at the counter.

COFFEE MANTRA

Map 2; Borgo La Croce 71r, Sant'Ambrogio; ///suspect.shave.decimal; 329 073 0808

This matchbox-sized café acts as a flagship for Gearbox Coffee Roasters, an ethical Tuscan start-up based north of the city. Come for a morning cappuccino with a difference, made with organic milk from restaurant Cibrèo's personal herd of cows, which ensures the best possible quality and creaminess.

JOHN BORNO

Map 2; Via Giuseppe Verdi 73/75r, Duomo; ///whites.pylons.beans; 055 906 7156

John Borno works for everyone. Like the visiting friend craving a cinnamon latte, not another espresso. Or the colleagues who want to smoke and chat on the tables that spill onto sunny Piazza Salvemini. Bonus: there's no table charge here.

CAFFÈ RONDINELLI

Map 1; Via dei Rondinelli 5r, Santa Maria Novella; ///dishing.steamed.attends; 055 230 2237

Minimally staffed and without much of a menu to speak of, Rondinelli isn't sexy. But on a road steeped in spectacle, just off fashion strip Via Tornabuoni, that's precisely its appeal. Cosy on in and knock back an afternoon espresso *al bar* with office workers on their breaks.

» Don't leave without making like an Italian schoolchild and grabbing a *merenda* (afternoon snack) to tide you over between meals.

Cocktail Joints

Florence may be the birthplace of the negroni, but it doesn't rests on its laurels. There's a long-standing reverence for the art of a well-mixed drink, with creative concoctions served in swanky settings.

MAD SOULS & SPIRITS

Map 3; Borgo San Frediano 36/38r, San Frediano;
///jigging.crawled.recline; www.madsoulsandspirits.com

Don't show up hungry: the committed cocktail purists who run this bar refuse to serve any food beyond the most basic pickles and bar nuts. You'll also risk getting booted out for requesting a vodka soda or Aperol Spritz, but it's all in the name of fun. MAD simply sticks to what it knows and loves – playfully titled and adventurous

Try it!
A WEEK OF TASTINGS

Visit during Florence Cocktail Week *(www. florencecocktailweek.it)* in September, when 25 or so of the top bars host masterclasses, tastings and after parties. Delicious non-alcoholic cocktails are served, too.

drinks. A sense of humour permeates the place, where jokes are written alongside the daily specials on a blackboard and charismatic mixologists deliver puns as they serve your cocktail.

LA MÉNAGÈRE

Map 4; Via dei' Giorni 8r, San Lorenzo; ///journals.bootleg.splits; www.lamenagere.it

French in name, La Ménagère is entirely Italian in practice. Chic girlfriends live for evenings spent under its high vaulted ceilings, sipping foamy pink cocktails in vintage crystal coupes and nibbling on sashimi. When everyone's caught up on the week's gossip, it's down to the basement bar to sway to sultry live jazz.

 » Don't leave without checking out the on-site florist. If you're someone's guest in Florence, a wildflower bouquet will go down a treat.

LOGGIA ROOF BAR

Map 3; Piazza Santo Spirito 9, Santo Spirito; ///spoon.slipping.bars; www.palazzoguadagni.com

Find the grand old wooden door for the Palazzo Guadagni Hotel and, inside, hop in a rickety lift up to the top floor. This is old-world Italy at its best: a magical rooftop bar overlooking one of Florence's vibiest piazzas, and a seriously atmospheric spot for a sundowner. Service is slow, but once you're reclined on a swing seat with a margarita on the way, it won't matter a jot. Book ahead to bag a table at sunset, when the rooftops glow a golden hue and the church bells across Florence chime in the distance.

RASPUTIN

Map 3; Borgo Tegolaio, Santo Spirito; www.rasputinsecretbar.com

Look up this secret, speakeasy-inspired spot online and you'll be vaguely directed towards a phone number that may or may not get answered. You're better off asking revellers in nearby Piazza Santo Spirito for directions, since this bar relies on word of mouth. Don't expect parties once you've rung the bell; with Prohibition-esque drinks, vintage furniture and candelabras, Rasputin prides itself on refinement. It's a quiet spot, yet there's a camaraderie in the shared seclusion.

GOSH*

Map 3; Via Santo Spirito 46r, Santo Spirito;
///sobered.polite.sectors; 345 934 2705

The Gin Basil may as well be the only drink on the menu at this bar: it's all anyone ever drinks, and it's the only place you'll find it. Of course, Gosh* is about so much more than the gin, lime and basil cocktail, delicious though it is. A night here may mean lingering on Via Santo Spirito chatting to the bartenders, or it may mean dancing to techno music till 4am, surrounded by pink flamingo wallpaper.

LOCALE

Map 2; Via delle Seggiole 12r, Duomo;
///heap.crystal.farms; www.localefirenze.it

There's a delicious dash of theatre to this decadent bar. In a former Medici palace, suave mixologists serve up bewitching cocktails that smoulder with dry ice or bubble with foam. Each creation provokes a dramatic gasp of awe from the Italian glitterati, who embody old-world glamour in their sequins and corsets – the unspoken dress code on the weekends. Off menu, ask for a passion fruit martini topped with chamomile foam – a drink reserved for those in the know – and sip it in the atrium.

» **Don't leave without** seeing if you can get a tour of the medieval dungeons, where Locale staff brew *kombucha* and herbal infusions.

ARTS INN
Map 4; Via del Porcellana 63r, Santa Maria Novella;
///pounding.dogs.tiny; www.theartsinn-florence.com

Florence is a city that loves art as much as a well-mixed drink, so artist Peter Thomas Foster was onto something when he opened this gallery/bar in his former atelier. As well as showcasing a permanent collection of Peter's work, Arts Inn hosts rotating exhibitions from various artists, accompanied by art-inspired drinks. Order the Frida K – a Mezcal- and chilli pepper-boosted negroni – and admire the brushstrokes of the paintings that line the walls.

Shh!

Order a whisky sour at Move On Record Store *(www.move onfirenze.com)* and head up to the first floor. Ask nicely and they'll let you perch on the tiny Juliet balcony, which has just enough space for two. It's your very own front row view of the Duomo and a perfect spot for an impromptu drink.

Wine Bars

Pardon the cliché, but wine is the lifeblood of Florence. Tuscany is world-famous for big hitters like Chianti, Bolgheri and Brunello di Montalcino, something Florentines are more than proud of.

PITTI GOLA E CANTINA

Map 3; Piazza de' Pitti 16, Santo Spirito; ///error.renews.scrap;
www.pittigolaecantina.com

"No water, just wine" declares the sign outside – a dash of Florentine humour directed at the tourists who pop in asking for bottles of water. But don't mistake this cheekiness for unfriendliness. While the setting is refined, with its Palazzo Pitti view, wine snobbery is unwelcome. Instead, there's a firm ethos that the best wine is the one you enjoy drinking the most; here, it'll likely be from a small Tuscan producer.

VINI E DELIZIE

Map 4; Via dei Banchi 45r, Santa Maria Novella;
///orbit.balance.snippet; 055 215 686

Since opening in 1973, family-run Vini e Delizie has been a haven for office workers winding down and weary travellers seeking a cheeseboard and a well-priced glass of Chianti. When the weather's right, casual sidewalk seating offers a straight-on look at Brunelleschi's orange-tiled dome, without the steep price tag typically attached to such a view.

» Don't leave without buying a bottle of one of the daily specials to take home. See what the regulars are picking up and follow suit.

LE VOLPI E L'UVA

Map 5; Piazza dei Rossi 1r, San Niccolò;
///spelling.episode.beaker; www.levolpieluva.com

Not many locals could locate blink-and-you'll-miss-it Piazza dei Rossi on a map, but tell them it's the square hosting this wine haunt and they'll know where you mean. Owners Riccardo, Ciro and Emilio source directly from winemakers across Tuscany, as well as the likes of Sardinia and Piedmont, and can share background on every bottle. That's the beauty of focusing on small, specialty producers, distinguishing Le Volpi e l'Uva from spots with lengthy, quasi-anonymous lists. Space is scarce, and tables quickly fill up with friends of the owners, so book ahead.

Try it!
TASTE A SUPERTUSCAN

Sampling Supertuscans – made using non-traditional grapes and methods – is a must. Take a day trip to Bolgheri and tour the Terre del Marchesato *(www.terredelmarchesato. com)* cellar before enjoying a glass.

Solo, Pair, Crowd

Wine is as important as water in Florence, so relaxing over a glass or a bottle is mandatory, regardless of the company (or not) you keep.

FLYING SOLO

Wine and dine yourself

Enoteca Fuori Porta in San Niccolò is all for offering fine wine within everyone's reach, so rest assured prices are reasonable and the staff are approachable. Each wine is paired with a delectable dish, too.

IN A PAIR

Celebrate with champagne

The Champagne Bar at The Place, a fancy hotel in Santa Maria Novella, was made for special occasions – just be sure to wear your finest and prepare to splash out.

FOR A CROWD

Cosy catch-ups

Family-run Enoteca Bellini in Santa Maria Novella might give off intimate date vibes, but the vaulted, thoroughly Tuscan back room is great for larger parties. Call ahead to book, then let the wine flow.

FIASCHETTERIA OSTERIA NUVOLI

Map 1; Piazza dell'Olio 15r, Duomo; ///curve.ashes.trailer; 055 2396 616

Dare ask for a coffee – or worse, a spritz – and you'll get a curt reply that wine has been served here since the 1800s. A mid-morning glass of red perched on Nuvoli's stoops and stools (in the shadow of the Duomo, no less) is a Florentine pastime, so settle in with the old boys and enjoy.

» Don't leave without loading up on snacks. The *crostini* (little toasts) are divine, topped with the likes of truffle and chicken liver.

CASA DEL VINO

Map 4; Via dell'Ariento 16r, San Lorenzo; ///narrow.slogans.fidget; www.casadelvino.it

The overstuffed stalls in the San Lorenzo market area can sometimes obscure the treasures behind them, like this tiny wood-clad bar. From late morning on, owner Gianni shares his knowledge on the best Tuscan wine and trades quips with workers breaking for lunch.

VINERIA SONORA

Map 2; Via degli Alfani 39r, Sant'Ambrogio; ///cold.elevate.habit; www.vineriasonora.it

A natural wine bar that wouldn't be out of place in Milan, this chic spot is a forward-thinking addition in a city where Chianti is all the rage. Vineria Sonora prides itself on an Italian collection of organic and biodynamic options, including funky orange wines. It's young and fresh, with vinyl spinning on a record player setting the tone.

Vino Sfuso and Takeaway Tipples

When you can share a bottle on your balcony or take a drink to the piazza, why sit in a bar? Here, **vini sfusi** *(where local wine is sold from barrels into reusable bottles) and bars offering cocktails to-go are prized.*

POP

**Map 3; Piazza Santo Spirito 18r, Santo Spirito;
///glider.copiers.presses; 055 217 475**

A classic Saturday night plan for any young Florentine in the mood for socializing is simply to "meet at Pop". This invariably means bumping into old friends and making new ones, sharing social media handles over a takeaway cocktail on the piazza.

IL SANTO VINO

**Map 3; Borgo Tegolaio 46r, Santo Spirito; ///press.alleges.courtyard;
055 538 7122**

It's a rite of passage to stop by this hole in the wall en route to a house party, battling through cobwebs to dispense wine from the barrel at around €4 a litre. It's not just budget-loving students who

Il Santo Vino also sells fresh-pressed olive oil in refillable bottles when in season, starting late October.

know about it, though. On Friday afternoons, folk with motorbike helmets under one arm and empty bottles under the other stock up for the weekend.

FIASCHETTERIA DELLE CURE
Map 6; Viale Volta 114, Le Cure; ///relaxed.rising.topping; www.lafiaschetteriadellecure.it

The leafy Le Cure neighbourhood just outside the city centre might be overlooked by tourists, but those who call it home passionately vouch for its great local bars. This low-key bottle shop and wine bar is a case in point, where the carefully selected wines change by the season, and can be filled in a variety of flagon sizes to take home.

» Don't leave without ordering a craft beer. There's a great selection both in bottles and on tap, if you'd like to sit in for a while.

BACCO NUDO
Map 2; Via dei Macci 59r, Sant'Ambrogio; ///scarred.selling.friends; 055 243 298

Named after the Roman God of wine, this popular "wine on tap" spot is Florence's self-proclaimed temple of *vino sfuso*. A visit here is always a pleasure, from consulting friendly owner Francesco on which wine to pick to watching him bottle and cork your purchase. He'll help you decide on your tipple based not only on what you're eating, but exactly how you're planning to cook it. Expect to come in seeking a Tuscan red only to leave with a sparkling variety.

Liked by the locals

"I come to Norcineria in Mercato Sant'Ambrogio for elegant Tuscan produce like *finocchiona* salami, *guanciale* (pork cheek) and pancetta, paired with cheese, bread and the beautiful wine on tap."

EDOARDO CELADON,
JOURNALIST

ENOTECA ALLA SOSTA DEI PAPI

**Map 2; Borgo la Croce 81r, Sant'Ambrogio; ///observe.bridge.informs;
www.sostadeipapi.it**

Plastic grapes hang in the entrance of this old-fashioned *vinaio* (wine
merchant), almost the last of a dying breed in Florence. Locals have
a deep affinity for sweet places like this, filling up their used wine bottles
from the barrels or sipping a dry red by the glass along the pavement.

KE CI METTO?

**Map 2; Borgo la Croce 52r, Piazza Beccaria, Sant'Ambrogio;
///awaiting.exams.weds; 329 592 1160**

This affordable spot is a well-kept secret among long-suffering
aperitivo-goers priced out of the city centre. The neon orange sign
can be spotted halfway along Borgo La Croce, advertising spritz
and negroni in take-away cups like a beacon for those wandering
towards a dinner reservation. Think of it as juice for your journey.
» Don't leave without ordering a *vin brûlée* (mulled wine) in winter
to warm you on your way down the cobblestone streets.

NORCINERIA E VINERIA DELLA C.BIO

Map 2; Mercato di Sant'Ambrogio, Sant'Ambrogio; ///kick.inflict.screamed

At this glorified market stall – one of late chef Fabio Picci's many
outposts in Florence – shoppers down their grocery bags to hunt for an
organic wine to pair with dinner. Try before you buy with a small glass
for a euro or two, along with a little truffle butter bun, then select the
bottle you want and have the staff fill it for you. Only open until 2pm.

An evening
wine window walk

Utterly unique to Florence, *buchette del vino* (wine windows) have been getting a lot of attention since the pandemic. These small holes in palace walls were used to sell surplus wine to the working classes in the 16th century, and proved ideal for touch-free contact during the plague. Though they fell into disuse over time, a handful were reopened during COVID-19 to dispense everything from coffee to spritz in a germ-free way. There's great pleasure in spotting a wine window as you amble around the city, even more so when your evening *vino* is served through one.

1. Via San Niccolò 79
Santa Croce
///sedated.waffle.migrate

2. Babae
Via Santo Spirito 21r, Santo
Spirito; www. babaefirenze.it
///teaches.salsa.droplet

3. Il Latini
Via dei Palchetti 6r, Santa
Maria Novella; 055 210 916
///tenders.interval.zoomed

4. Vivoli
Via dell'Isola delle Stinche 7r,
Santa Croce; www.vivoli.it
///resort.boxing.surreal

Wine Windows Association ///pursuit.helpless.running

Via dei Martelli 9 ///punch.elevated.tempting

Enjoy an aperitivo at
BABAE

This restaurant was the first to revive the wine window tradition in 2019, before the pandemic hit. Go for the daily wine hour (7–8pm), ask for a glass of red and sip it streetside with the locals.

Arno

Ponte alla Carraia

BORGO SAN FREDIANO

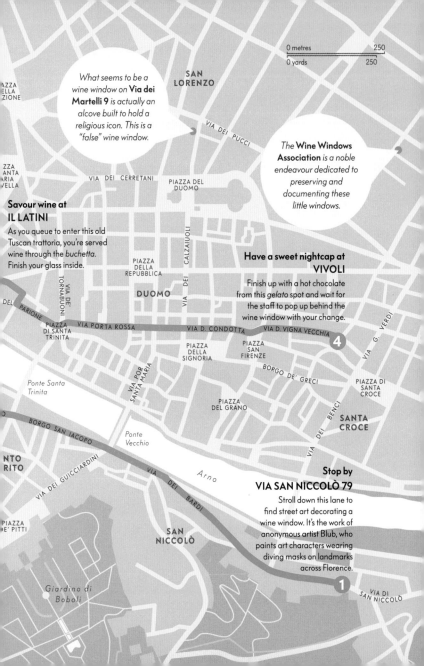

*What seems to be a wine window on **Via dei Martelli 9** is actually an alcove built to hold a religious icon. This is a "false" wine window.*

*The **Wine Windows Association** is a noble endeavour dedicated to preserving and documenting these little windows.*

Savour wine at
IL LATINI

As you queue to enter this old Tuscan trattoria, you're served wine through the *buchetta*. Finish your glass inside.

Have a sweet nightcap at
VIVOLI

Finish up with a hot chocolate from this *gelato* spot and wait for the staff to pop up behind the wine window with your change.

Stop by
VIA SAN NICCOLÒ 79

Stroll down this lane to find street art decorating a wine window. It's the work of anonymous artist Blub, who paints art characters wearing diving masks on landmarks across Florence.

SAN LORENZO

VIA DEI PUCCI

VIA DEI CERRETANI

PIAZZA DEL DUOMO

VIA DEI CALZAIUOLI

PIAZZA DELLA REPUBBLICA

DUOMO

VIA DEI TORNABUONI

DEL PARIONE

PIAZZA DI SANTA TRINITA

VIA PORTA ROSSA

VIA D. CONDOTTA

VIA D. VIGNA VECCHIA

VIA G. VERDI

PIAZZA DELLA SIGNORIA

PIAZZA SAN FIRENZE

BORGO DE' GRECI

PIAZZA DI SANTA CROCE

Ponte Santa Trinita

VIA POR SANTA MARIA

PIAZZA DEL GRANO

VIA DEL BENCI

SANTA CROCE

BORGO SAN IACOPO

Ponte Vecchio

Arno

NTO RITO

VIA DEI GUICCIARDINI

VIA DEI BARDI

SAN NICCOLÒ

PIAZZA DE' PITTI

Giardino di Boboli

VIA DI SAN NICCOLÒ

0 metres 250
0 yards 250

SHOP

If the "effortless Italian elegance" stereotype holds up anywhere, it's Florence, which has the shopping scene and head-turning local style to prove it.

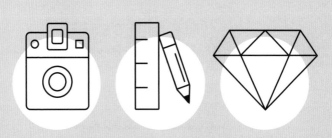

Artisanal Jewellery

Florence's jewellery heritage extends way beyond flashy goldsmiths on the Ponte Vecchio. Rather than buying bling from big brands, locals are more likely to own a special piece made by passionate artisans.

ANGELA CAPUTI

Map 3; Via Santo Spirito 58r, Santo Spirito; ///informs.waxing.shipped; www.angelacaputi.com

Angela Caputi's designs are as colour-saturated as any Mannerist painting, and she's just as iconic (the bus stop near this flagship shop is named for her). With her signature chunky jewellery draped around her neck, Angela still assembles Hollywood-inspired collections at the back of this shop, her bold brooches and earrings a break from the elegant but staid style that the city tends to default to.

LE ARTI ORAFE

Map 3; Via dei Serragli 104, San Frediano; ///players.rams.worked; www.artiorafe.it

Though apprenticing in workshops is a long Tuscan tradition, Le Arti Orafe (LAO) was the first local institution of its kind when it opened in 1985 – a school dedicated to the art of jewellery making. This is where the jewellers of tomorrow buff metal and set stones, and you can view and buy their wares if you book an appointment. Who knows – you might just walk away with a piece from the next Angela Caputi.

FRATELLI PERUZZI

Map 5; Ponte Vecchio 60, San Niccolò; ///router.patting.saints; www.fratelliperuzzi.com

There's no time quite like early morning on the Ponte Vecchio, when goldsmiths open their workshops and couples start to eye up antique rings. While gold is the medium that dominates on this historic bridge, silver leads the way at Fratelli, now run by fourth-generation metalsmiths. Expect to shop alongside well-tailored gentlemen after new cufflinks and elegant hostesses looking for candelabras.

» Don't leave without browsing the collection that honours the Jewish tradition, including intricate mezuzahs and Torah pointers.

GRIMALDO FIRENZE

Map 3; Via Maggio 10r, Santo Spirito; ///lizards.hulk.bubbles; www.grimaldofirenze.com

Grimaldo's timeless goods – the likes of diamond bands and stacked stone rings – fit firmly into Italian family heirloom territory. These days, however, most young locals come to Grimaldo to buy lifetime necklaces or earrings from Lady Ripple. This brand has created a buzz with its bee-themed collection, with 10 per cent of all proceeds going towards the Bee the Ripple initiative, supporting organic urban beekeeping in Florence.

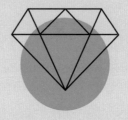

Liked by the locals

"Florence is one of the main centres of Italian craftsmanship. My view is that one always has to try to keep craftsmanship as something on the edge, separate from commercial norms, to allow the artisan to live more like an artist."

ANGELA CAPUTI, JEWELLERY DESIGNER

LA GAZZA LADRA GIOIELLI

Map 2; Piazza Gaetano Salvemini 6, Sant'Ambrogio;
///womb.snapper.reacting; www.lagazzaladragioielli.com

Given Florence's artisanal legacy, jewellery here can be expensive. This boutique swaps showy and pricey for classic and understated, with gold-plated rings, pendants and earrings in the €40–60 range.

» **Don't leave without** browsing pieces with the fleur-de-lis symbol, the stylized lily linked with French royalty but now an emblem of Florence.

NOKIKE ATELIER

Map 3; Via dei Serragli 122r, San Frediano; ///wing.dandelions.goats;
www.nokike.com

Owner Herika Signorino is just as cheery and eclectic as the rings, necklaces, barrettes and other bling at her atelier. Herika's background in web design and graphics informs her geometric and playful designs – as irresistible to her loyal clientele as her rescue pup Nilla is, who tends to nuzzle up to you for a pat while you browse.

ALESSANDRO DARI

Map 5; Via di San Niccolò 115r, San Niccolò; ///slippers.rankings.shack;
www.alessandrodari.com

Alessandro Dari's imaginative studio resembles a witch's lair, complete with bubbling cauldrons and whistling flames. The enigmatic designer's approach to his jewellery is steampunk; his shop's music and lighting, moody. All the pomp is hard to ignore, but so are the otherworldly (and wallet-draining) designs themselves.

Beauty Buys

A simple yet intentional beauty routine is as sacred as any Renaissance chapel in Florence. Treat yourself to the products that Florentines can't live without at these long-standing perfumeries and pharmacies.

AQUAFLOR

Map 2; Borgo Santa Croce 6, Santa Croce; ///saloons.migrants.quieter; www.aquaflor.it

It might be hidden in the shadow of Santa Croce, but the scents of iris and sandalwood emanating from this perfumery help people find their way. Inside, staff spritz colognes for customers on the shop floor while resident "nose" Nicola Bianchi works in the basement lab, dreaming up bespoke scents for those willing to pay the price.

Try it!
SHAPE YOUR SCENT

Book a *profumoir* appointment at Sileno Cheloni Maestro Profumiere (*www. silenocheloni.com*) and create a made-to-measure 100 ml fragrance with perfumer Sileno himself.

Whether you splash out to design your own perfume or buy a €48 room diffuser for your living room, the fragrance will be something unexpected. In short, this isn't the place to come for a standard jasmine scent to gift your mum.

OFFICINA DE' TORNABUONI

Map 1; Via de' Tornabuoni 19n, Santa Maria Novella;
///paints.clauses.iron; www.odtskincare.com

Given its location on Florence's high-end shopping street, Officina de' Tornabuoni tempts international shoppers with expensive tastes (they've most likely just had a glass of champagne at nearby Procacci, *p136*). Here, they stop in to restock their staple skincare supplies, leaving with rejuvenating eye creams, lip balms, toners and body fragrances – all natural and handcrafted in Tuscany.

FARMACIA MÜNSTERMANN

Map 4; Piazza Carlo Goldoni 6, Santa Maria Novella;
///central.price.streaks; www.munstermann.it

It was German pharmacist Münstermann who first brought homeopathy to Florence in 1897, and his founding pharmacy still feels delightfully trapped in time. Antique cabinets and wooden countertops overflow with soaps, shaving creams and primping tools, all made on-site. It's hard to imagine the chemists keeping their products catalogued on any system but parchment paper.

» Don't leave without buying a retro chic tote bag, emblazoned with the Münstermann logo, to take your cosmetics home in.

FARMACIA SANTISSIMA ANNUNZIATA

Map 4; Via dei Servi 80, San Marco; ///succeed.snuggle.pebbles;
www.farmaciassannunziata1561.it

This pharmacy might be stark and small, but its products are just as desirable as those in any lavish shop. The buttery-soft hand cream is the most coveted product, tucked into handbags during Florence's brisk winters or sitting atop bathroom shelves to soothe tired skin.

OFFICINA PROFUMO-FARMACEUTICA DI SANTA MARIA NOVELLA

Map 4; Via Della Scala 16, Santa Maria Novella;
///downward.snow.conquest; www.eu.smnnovella.com

When Dominican friars founded Santa Maria Novella in the 13th century, caretaking for the garden became a key part of monastic life. Slowly, the monks began creating herbal remedies, and as news started to spread of their potions, a pharmacy – Europe's oldest – was

Shh!

With no storefront, fragrance laboratory Arômantique *(www. aromantique.it)* manages to be hidden in Sant'Ambrogio. Run by the charismatic Maria Letizia Longo, an ex-architect who uncovered a hidden passion for aromatherapy, the space has an idyllic garden and hosts DIY workshops on the likes of home diffusers, essential oils, perfumes and potpourri.

opened in 1621. The formulas created by the monks are still honoured today, so while the brand's status has grown worldwide and sees hordes of tourists enter the shop's frescoed folds, a whiff of the iconic rose water or Tuscan potpourri will take you right back to the 1200s.

» **Don't leave without** exploring the building with its old chapel (now the main sales room), its frescoed sacristy and its tearoom.

SPEZIERIE PALAZZO VECCHIO

Map 1; Via Vacchereccia 9r, Duomo; ///noisy.bigger.mainland; www.spezierepalazzovecchio.it

Italian noblewoman Caterina Sforza de' Medici was the first to write a recipe book of scented waters in the 1400s, and this apothecary-style shop honours her in the best way it knows how: a perfume. And she's not the only one celebrated here. Other Florentine figures and locations inspire the cosmetics, like the Giardino di Boboli spray made with the flowers and herbs found in the garden's grounds.

BOUTIQUE MUSEO LORENZO VILLORESI

Map 5; Via de' Bardi 12r, San Niccolò; ///steroids.talkers.spice; www.museovilloresi.it

For perfumer Lorenzo, aromas induce memories, be it a wood smell that carries you to your grandpa's bathroom cabinet or a lavender that whisks you to the Tuscan hills. His boutique and olfactory museum is built on this power of scent, where a "fragrance library" holds essences and spices collected on his trips around the globe, and a hidden garden grows citruses used to produce the perfumes for sale.

Made in Florence

Florentines know that true luxury isn't spending out on a glittery logo, but having something handcrafted. This is a city where artisans have been chipping away at their crafts for centuries, after all.

STEFANO BEMER

Map 5; Via di San Niccolò 2, San Niccolò; ///snares.curvy.slip; www.stefanobemer.com

It's a cliché, but it's true: Italian men have impeccable taste in shoes, including the late shoemaker Stefano Bemer. His legacy of exacting attention to detail lives on in this neighbourhood atelier, where craftspeople work on bespoke orders while you shop, manipulating python skins or handmaking heels on workbenches. A custom pair is a huge investment, but nothing completes a look like an Italian brogue.

RICCARDO BARTHEL

Map 3; Via dei Serragli 234r, San Frediano; ///closer.fills.shocks; www.riccardobarthel.it

It's the little details that make a house a home, like the floral tiles in your kitchen or the porcelain soap holder in your bathroom. These touches are where Riccardo Barthel excels. In a secluded courtyard,

Check out Desinare, the cooking school upstairs. Classes are in Italian, but the space is worth seeing.

bronzers and restorers beetle away creating tap fittings and door handles while locals browse the showrooms, soaking up ideas for their rental flats.

FRAU LEMAN

Map 3; Via della Chiesa 21r, Santo Spirito;
///stutter.crush.served; www.frauleman.com

The collaborative process between maker and customer is what sets Frau Leman apart. Using Italian leather that's been cast off by fashion houses, Berlin-trained artisan and owner Stephanie crafts bags and accessories in her workroom and shop. Standard designs are kept in stock, but the joy is in buying a made-to-order piece, choosing your lining fabric and waiting for the finished item to arrive in the post.

SOGNI IN CARTA

Map 4; Via Nazionale 43, Santa Maria Novella; ///blaze.stocky.meanest;
www.sogniincarta.com

The art of marbled paper dates back to the Middle Ages in Florence, when bookbinders would pass days floating colour on water before transferring the pattern onto paper. The practice is less common now, but the Vivani family have been keeping "Dreams in Paper" alive at this shop since 1926. The patterned paper works wonderfully for gift wrapping, while the postcards make divine thank you notes.

» Don't leave without picking up a leather photo album, bound by hand in calf leather, to fill with memories of your time in Florence.

EFG GUANTI

Map 4; Via della Spada 28r, Santa Maria Novella; ///finely.eggs.palaces;
www.efgguanti.it

Gloves have long been a sign of elegance in Italy, be it elbow-length
designs worn to the opera or embroidered patterns favoured by the
aristocracy. While leather has become the go-to material, EFG Guanti
also stocks a variety of hand-sewn pieces in soft fabrics. In a shop that's
as snug as a glove itself, classy owner Elena is on hand to advise on
the best shape, whether it's a silk-lined "Antonella" or pebbled "Dante".

SBIGOLI TERRECOTTE

Map 2; Via Sant'Egidio 4, Duomo; ///action.definite.snail;
www.sbigoliterrecotte.it

With clay clinging to their hair, Sbigoli's mother-daughter ceramicist
duo shape, fire and decorate all items in this workshop, wiping
their hands on their dusty aprons to greet shoppers. Lining the shelves
and walls are everything you'd find in an Italian mamma's dining room
cabinet – mugs, mixing bowls, party trays – all hand-painted in riffs
on 15th-century European designs or olive-speckled patterns.

BENHEART

Map 4; Via della Vigna Nuova 18r, Santa Maria Novella;
///humidity.handbook.cycled; www.benheart.it

Morocco-born Ben's desire to create a leather jacket collection began
when he moved to Italy – famous for its leather production – as a child.
Yet it was only after a heart transplant at the age of 29 that he was

driven to fulfil this dream. With childhood friend Matteo, Ben opened a store in Florence – a city where a leather jacket never goes out of style. Be it a strong biker look or a soft bohemian cut, each handcrafted jacket is a solid investment piece.

» **Don't leave without** browsing the accessories. The belts, shoes and wallets – all made with leather – pair well with a staple jacket purchase.

SCUOLA DEL CUOIO

Map 2; Via San Giuseppe 5r, Santa Croce; ///lobby.replays.wiping; www.scuoladelcuoio.it

In a monastery behind Santa Croce church, artisans cut belts beneath frescoes, the clang of church bells the only intrusion of the outside world. This is the renowned Scuola del Cuoio: part school, part leather goods shop. When poverty hit the city in the wake of World War II, local artisans came together with Franciscan friars to found a leather institution that would teach orphans a trade. The educational side continues today (though instead of orphans, it's adults doing the learning), with some of the work on offer in the small showroom.

Try it!
TOUR A TANNERY

Book a guided visit at Scuola del Cuoio. You'll learn about the school's history, the different leather techniques and skins, and the two collections produced in the workshops.

Gourmet Treats

Grocery shopping in Florence is less about splurging and more about picking up simple, high-quality ingredients as needed – a bottle of olive oil, say, or a bunch of fresh herbs.

LA BOTTEGA DELLA FRUTTA

Map 4; Via de' Federighi 31, Santa Maria Novella; ///wolf.trooper.tidying; 055 239 8590

This stuffed-to-the-brim boutique is a relief from the odd shoves and queue-jumps often encountered in the city's larger supermarkets. Here, couple and owners Elisabetta and Francesco are always ready with a tip on what produce is freshest that day. Consider this a lovely little place to pick up wines, cheeses and vegetables for holiday homecooking or picnics.

PEGNA DAL 1860

Map 1; Via dello Studio 26r, Duomo; ///pavement.asserts.reach; www.pegna.sangiustosrl.com

Loyal customers still remember the days when they visited this shop with their parents, unwrapping a candy while mamma browsed the aisles. Trimmings of the past define this grocery store, located on the ground floor of a converted 17th-century monastery. Lining dark wooden cabinets are iconic Italian products by region – Krumiri Rossi biscuits from Piedmont, salted capers from Sicily, white truffles from Tuscany – in old-school packaging.

MIGONE CONFETTI

Map 1; Via dei Calzaiuoli 85r, Piazza della Repubblica, Duomo; ///debater.serious.pumpkin; 055 214 004

Try not to knock over shoppers balancing trays of candies: they're likely picking up wedding favours. This Italian tradition typically involves giving guests sugar-coated almonds in tied bags, and soon-to-be-married locals rely on Migone for this. If you're in need of a gift for your host, the cakes in beautiful packaging shaped like the Baptistery or Duomo are some of Migone's trademarks (they're tastefully done, a far cry from those found in made-for-tourist shops.)
» Don't leave without picking out some sweets for yourself from the retro glass jars, filled with bonbons, marzipan, sherbet and liquorice.

Shh!

Florentine gourmands joke about having a truffle dealer on speed dial, and you'll wish you did too after trying the white truffles sold by Truffle Italia. Truffle hunter Tommaso

Inghrami sells directly from the Tuscan countryside to the best restaurants in Italy, as well as to truffle-loving individuals (when supplies allow). Email him at info@truffle-italia.com.

Solo, Pair, Crowd

Whether it's a peaceful market stroll or a trip to buy some cheese and wine with pals, Florence always tastes good.

FLYING SOLO
Pick up some pasta
Mercato Sant'Ambrogio is the king of gourmet pasta – the kind you won't want to share. Choose between the likes of handmade tortelli stuffed with pear and ricotta or artichokes and lemon then cook up a solo feast at home.

IN A PAIR
Shop and sip
Part wine cellar, part high-end grocery, Alessi in the Duomo area is the place to find a smorgasbord of Italian goods. Stock up on almond *cantuccini* for date night before enjoying a glass of wine at the bar.

FOR A CROWD
Wine time
Enoteca (wine shop and bar) Fratelli Zanobini in San Lorenzo is designated a "historic locale of Florence" for its excellent selection of Tuscan bottles. Gather your friends and order a few bottles to share.

BUONAMICI BOTTEGA

**Map 3; Via dell'Orto 31/33r, San Frediano; ///situated.issued.drove;
www.buonamiciabottega.ecwid.com**

When residents of sleepy San Frediano can't make it to morning food
markets, Buonamici is there for their pantry staple needs. Before
stocking up on fresh pesto, heritage grain pastas and organic eggs,
locals scrabble for the last coveted chocolate panettone: a three-
day labour of love made in Buonamici's pastry lab next door.

L'OLANDESE VOLANTE

**Map 4; Via San Gallo 44r, San Marco; ///quiz.captures.canines;
www.lolandesevolante.webs.com**

Mild-mannered Janse keeps things quirky in The Flying Dutchman,
with Dutch specialities stocked among kitsch antique objects. In one
corner, you might find Buddha statues lining the counter above Edam
cheese; in another, childhood toys keeping guard over bonbons.

I BALLERINI

**Map 6; Borgo Ognissanti 132r, Santa Maria Novella;
///tidying.foiled.actor; www.cioccolateriaballerini.it**

Tuscan food is best when fresh, but this means nothing to your mother
demanding Italian treats be bought home. The seasonal sweets at
this chocolate shop travel surprisingly well, so build a confectionary
box of dried fruits and speckled white chocolates to keep her happy.
» Don't leave without having lunch in the back corner, where staff
serve fresh pizza slices made on crisp and salty *schiacciata* crust.

Street Style

True Florentine style is based on sophistication, never ostentation. Outfits rely on a capsule wardrobe of timeless staples, with the odd statement piece thrown in to add personality.

FLY – FASHION LOVES YOU STORE

Map 2; Borgo Pinti, 20r, Sant'Ambrogio; ///yell.removed.inflict; www.fashionlovesyou.it

Wide-eyed students come to Florence with a dream: to learn from the masters at Europe's most prestigious fashion schools. Shopping at this cute concept store, run through Florence University of the Arts (FUA), is a brilliant way to support such dreams, picking up unique garments created by fashion students. Artisanal and niche brands are stocked here, too.

BJØRK

Map 3; Via dello Sprone 25r, Santo Spirito; ///floating.odds.encoder; www.bjork-florence.com

When Filippo Anzalone returned to his home town after a stint in London, he was underwhelmed by Florence's old-school attitude. Bjørk was his response to Renaissance city clichés, including the tendency to hover around the browsing customer. With seating throughout the boutique, Bjørk invites clients to linger as they decide which flowing linen dress suits their colouring best and if that slinky shirt they've tried on is airy enough.

» **Don't leave without** leafing through the hard-to-find-in-Florence design magazines (not for sale) like *Kinfolk* and *AnOther*.

HEART TO HEART IN FLORENCE

Map 3; Via Santo Spirito 54r, Santo Spirito; ///urge.image.revival; 333 644 1944

Sisters Giulia and Sara opened this concept store in their father's former rug shop, A&L Tappeti, in 2018. The silk change purses here are darling, but it's the velvet Venetian slippers (loafers, not the house shoe kind) that are a Florentine favourite, paired with jeans for a lazy spring walk or a fancy dress for a black-tie event. Pick your pair – perhaps a bright red, a forest green or a deep blue – before getting it customized with kitsch embroidery.

TICHE CLOTHING

Map 4; Via San Zanobi 122r, San Lorenzo; ///painting.slug.sound; www.ticheclothing.com

Florentine women have an affinity for elegant self-expression, and Tiche's understated clothes reflect this. A "less is more" approach defines designer Tijana Stanković's pieces, her signatures being twill trousers and breezy cotton dresses in muted neutrals or subtle florals, perfect for breezing down the cobbled streets.

OTTOD'AME

Map 4; Via della Spada 19r, Santa Maria Novella;
///dial.limbs.steps; www.ottodame.it

A lot of local labels get by doing one wardrobe staple incredibly well: leather jackets, painterly scarves, designer dark sunglasses. This whimsical born-in-Florence brand, however, somehow manages to do everything – and provide for every occasion – perfectly. Viscose two-piece set for a wedding weekend in Tuscany? *Si.* Sparkly statement dress for a public speaking engagement? Naturally. Tartan wool trousers for market-hopping on an autumnal Saturday? In at least three colour palettes. Half the joy is checking back with each calendar event, as the colourful displays rotate nearly as often as the area's *ristorante* specials.

» Don't leave without browsing the CARING collection, which is committed to producing sustainable garments, sustainably.

SAGLIANO CONCETTI SARTORIALI

Map 3; Borgo San Frediano 47r, San Frediano;
///cheered.sponsors.outreach; www.saglianoconcettisartoriali.com

A menswear tailor in the Neapolitan tradition, Sagliano is the place that outfits genteel guys on their afternoon *passeggiata*. You know the kind: they're equally at home on a piazza bench or in magazine spreads espousing classic Florentine elegance. They feel just as content in this store, owned by tailor Rosario, who comes from a family where thread and thimble have always brought the bread and butter. Every fairly priced suit is made to measure and requires an appointment with Rosario, who oversees each garment himself.

Liked by the locals

"In Florence, the myth-like Pitti peacocks (the gentlemen who attend the Pitti Uomo fashion fair) match high-quality tailored suits with irreverent accessories such as brooches, rings, bow ties and pocket squares."

ALESSANDRO MASETTI, FOUNDER OF THE
FASHION COMMENTATOR BLOG

Vintage Gems

While most locals buy their wardrobe essentials new, ask where they found their fur coat or luxe designer handbag and the answer will invariably be a vintage boutique or market (if not nonna's closet).

MERCATO DELLE CASCINE

Map 6; Viale dei Lecci, Cascine Park, Porta al Prato; ///mailbox.drainage.modules

Every Tuesday at the crack of dawn, traders set up their wares along the portion of Cascine Park that backs onto the Arno. By 9am, the stretch is filled with Florentines on a mission, bouquets of flowers peeping out of their bags as they rifle for cashmere jumpers. If you've eyed a vintage fur coat, prepare to roll up your sleeves and jostle with bargain-hunting nonnas, amped up on the smell of mothballs.

MERCATO SANT'AMBROGIO

Map 2; Piazza Lorenzo Ghiberti, Sant'Ambrogio; ///noses.develops.dishes; 055 248 0778

Though the quality of the second-hand clothes on the outdoor stalls here aren't as high as the produce sold in the covered market, the Sant'Ambrogio community converges here regardless, bargaining

Head here early – the best deals are found on Thursday and Saturday mornings, and most vendors close up by 2pm.

with vendors over high-street turtlenecks and label-less jackets. Swing by the stall dedicated solely to vintage buttons to accessorize and upcycle your finds and they'll feel good as new.

RECOLLECTION DI ALBRICI

Map 3; Via dei Serragli 22r, Santo Spirito; ///decreased.curving.pointer; 055 211095

It's not just the vintage *haute couture* that makes this shop so appealing. Old copies of *Harper's Bazaar* are strewn artfully on coffee tables, ivy hangs from giant chandeliers and natural light floods the room. It's a lovely space to strut around in a Gucci two-piece, Hermes scarf and 1980s Chanel bag, posing in front of long, ornate mirrors before deciding which piece to invest in.

» Don't leave without picking out a pair of shoes to go with your outfit. Sparkly and embroidered heels line the walls neatly.

DESII VINTAGE

Map 1; Via dei Conti 17, Duomo; ///rash.manuals.think; www.desiifirenze.it

Italian style is synonymous with high-end brands, but achieving such a luxe look comes at a price. Desii ensures that heads will turn on your *passeggiata* without sacrificing your rent money. Nearly every vintage item for sale has been selected by owner Leonardo during his trips around the world: Gucci bags, Adidas and Reebok jumpers, and at least one item from every Louis Vuitton collection.

MELROSE VINTAGE STORE

Map 4; Largo Fragelli Alinari 40, Santa Maria Novella;
///sunshine.hushed.radar; 055 267 0030

In a city that proudly protects its past, Melrose Vintage Store fits like a pre-loved Chanel glove. If you're seeking said gloves (or any vintage designer brands), you'll find solace at the sister store in Via de Ginori. This spot in Alinari, meanwhile, presents like a timeline of fashion history, with flapper dresses sharing space with 1980s biker jackets.

» **Don't leave without** buying by weight: for around €40, you'll leave with 30 kg (66 lb) of vintage clothes from a host of eras.

TARTAN VINTAGE

Map 4; Via dei Palchetti 5a, Santa Maria Novella; ///owns.polite.tangible;
339 562 1310

Retro British style is surprisingly popular among a certain ilk of young professionals, who often sport Barbour jackets and chinos as they saunter down Via Tornabuoni. This vintage treasure chest helps them achieve a 1950s and 60s English look, stocking floral tea dresses, brass-buttoned velvet jackets, wool trousers and old-school peacoats.

A RITROSO... A REBOURS

Map 2; Via Ghibellina 24r, Sant'Ambrogio; ///roof.onto.thick;
www.vintage-firenze.it

This is not a "take your torn Levis and leave" sort of shop – once here you can't help but pause to hear all about the latest stock. Owner Camilla is a weaver of wardrobe narratives, and can tell the story behind almost every piece that she sources, be they fineries from around Europe or cast-offs from Florence's chicest individuals. Her passion is contagious, and she'll take all vintage hunters seriously, even if you aren't tip to toe in labels.

MERCATINO DEI NINNI

Map 4; Via de' Federighi 11r, Santa Maria Novella;
///standing.pens.jumpy; www.mercatinodininni.it

Many vintage shops survive on the "thrill of the hunt": the customer's dedication to uncovering buried treasure in overrun racks. Ninni is no such place. For one thing, the understated, elegant mammas who shop here wouldn't dare be seen ferociously upturning piles of clothing. For another, Ninni – named after the proprietor who runs the show, with help from her daughter – is more curated than most Florentine art exhibitions. No item here is an accident: dresses, suits, jackets, shoes and accessories are sourced from Ninni's lengthy Rolodex of contacts across Europe. Expect YSL, Chanel, Fendi and Prada as well as smaller contemporary brands.

Try it!
FIND YOUR FIT

Take a fashion walking tour with Alice Cozzi (*www.florencefashiontour.com*), who will guide you around some lesser-known thrift stores before a trip to her personal tailor to fit your new clothes perfectly.

SAN
LORENZO

PIAZZA
DI SANTA
MARIA
NOVELLA

Loretta Caponi *is
famous for having
dressed Sting, Madonna
and Princess Diana. Her
atelier is dedicated to
the art of embroidery.*

**Browse the stock at
LUISAVIAROMA**

Enjoy the fanciful displays
at this multi-brand concept
store, where global labels
like Alexander McQueen
share space with Italian
designers like Gucci.

PIAZZA SAN
GIOVANNI

SANTA
MARIA
NOVELLA

VIA DELLE BELLE DONNE

VIA DELLA SPADA

VIA ROMA

2

**Kick back at
PROCACCI**

Order truffle panini and champagne
(or a coffee) at this glamorous café. It
sells giftable jars of spreads, too.

3

VIA DEGLI STROZZI

PIAZZA
DELLA
REPUBBLICA

VIA D.
SPEZIALI

VI

*Major fashion
boutiques and the
Florence campus for
Istituto Marangoni
are found along*
Via de' Tornabuoni.

PIAZZA
DEGLI
STROZZI

VIA DE' TORNABUONI

VIA CALIMALA

VIA DEI CALZAIUOLI

DUOMO

VIA

PIAZZA
DI SANTA
TRINITA

**Walk the halls of the
MUSEO SALVATORE
FERRAGAMO**

4

VIA DELLE TERME

VIA
VACCHERECCIA

PIAZZ
DELL
SIGNO

Check out the sketches
and shoe models designed
by the famed Italian
creator Ferragamo at this
small museum.

LUNGARNO D. ACCIAIOLI

VIA POR SANTA MARIA

Arno

0 metres   100
0 yards   100

BORGO SAN IACOPO

*Ponte
Vecchio*

A day of
Florentine fashion

While business-focused Milan is Italy's global fashion capital, Florence is its sartorial soul. Luxury brands like Gucci and Pucci have their roots in Florence and it's here, too, that entrepreneur Giovanni Battista Giorgini hosted the first Italian high-fashion show, in 1951. In so doing, he challenged the monopoly of Paris's ateliers and helped to cement Italy as a fashion capital in the popular imagination. People have been talking about Italian fashion ever since, so join the discussion and soak up the city's style.

**Relive history at
ARCHIVIO STORICO FOTO LOCCHI**
Find inspiration for your next outfit at this archive, where the history of Tuscan fashion from the 1930s is documented through rare photos.

**Dine in style at
GUCCI OSTERIA**
Indulge in a swanky dinner of Italian classics at this high-fashion *osteria*, next to the Gucci Garden.

1. Archivio Storico Foto Locchi
Via del Corso 21r, Duomo; www.fotolocchi.it
///flute.plotting.salt

2. LUISAVIAROMA
Via Roma 19/21r, Duomo; www.luisaviaroma.com
///sending.downward.isolated

3. Procacci
Via de' Tornabuoni 64r, Duomo; www.procacci1885.it
///bicker.olive.painting

4. Museo Salvatore Ferragamo
Piazza di Santa Trinita 5r, Duomo; www.ferragamo.com/museo
///disposal.surveyed.arming

5. Gucci Osteria
Piazza della Signoria 10, Duomo; www.gucciosteria.com
///spike.weekends.pinks

Loretta Caponi
///pickle.prelude.hugs

DEI PUCCI

PROCONSOLO

VIA DEL

PIAZZA DI SAN FIRENZE

ARTS & CULTURE

Cradle of the Renaissance, the birthplace of opera, the home of high fashion: you don't need us to tell you that Florence hinges on culture and creativity.

Renaissance Relics

Oh, to live in the birthplace of the Renaissance.
The city's artistic legacy is a source of pride for
Florentines, who delight in classic collections housed
in grand palaces and fawn over intricate architecture.

CAPPELLE MEDICEE

Map 1; Piazza di Madonna degli Aldobrandini 6, San Lorenzo;
///lamps.workshops.liver; www.bargellomusei.beniculturali.it

The Medici lavished their wealth on many buildings in Florence, including their own two-part mausoleum. In the Chapel of the Princes, the Grand Dukes were laid to rest in sumptuous style, with expensive jasper, marble and coral decorating the walls. The New Sacristy tombs, meanwhile, were designed by Michelangelo, complete with beautiful sculptures. It's Medici vanity at its finest.

PALAZZO PITTI

Map 3; Piazza de' Pitti 1, Santo Spirito; ///cattle.observe.glider; www.uffizi.it

Originally built for banker Luca Pitti, the Palazzo Pitti became a city emblem when the Medici bought it for their royal residence in 1550. Over the centuries, new generations would amass paintings and porcelain within its walls: collections that now fill the five museums

Walk the famed Vasari Corridor, a raised system of hidden walkways that connect Palazzo Pitti to Palazzo Vecchio.

in this complex. Designers are evangelical about the Museum of Costume and Fashion and its garments dating from the 16th century, while artists favour the Palatine Gallery's world-class Titians.

PALAZZO MEDICI RICCARDI

Map 1; Via Camillo Cavour 3r, Duomo; ///undulation.bracelet.voice; www.palazzomediciriccardi.it

If the Medici were to return to Florence today, they'd see much of the city's skyline – which their wealthy rule helped to build and embellish – unchanged. Erected in 1444, this austere palace was the prototype for all Renaissance architecture that followed, and remains a calling card for those who go misty-eyed at Florence's elegant buildings.

» Don't leave without visiting the Magi Chapel, which served as a private place for prayer when the Medici lived here.

MUSEO NAZIONALE DEL BARGELLO

Map 1; Via del Proconsolo 4, Duomo; ///approve.worth.reacting; www.bargellomusei.beniculturali.it

When Donatello cast his bronze *David* in the 1440s, he created the first free-standing nude since antiquity, developing a "Renaissance style" that gave rise to a city-wide passion for sculpture. The Bargello is devoted to the fine sculptures that followed, with rooms for the likes of Giambologna and Cellini. Donatello's *David* might not be fawned over like Michelangelo's, but you'll at least have a quieter moment with it.

LE GALLERIE DEGLI UFFIZI

Map 1; Piazzale degli Uffizi 6, Duomo; ///duty.blizzard.goggle; www.uffizi.it

It's a local in-joke that many born-and-bred Florentines never set foot in the Uffizi until their forties. As the chief repository of Renaissance works (Botticelli, Leonardo, Titian), it has a touristy status that many refuse to indulge. When locals do decide to visit, it's usually on the first free Sunday of the month, or for the odd performance art piece – an initiative from director Eike Schmidt to reel in more residents.

GALLERIA DELL'ACCADEMIA

Map 4; Via Ricasoli 58/60, San Marco; ///palaces.pumpkin.silence; www.galleriaaccademiafirenze.it

Ah, *David*: he's Florence's "Golden Boy", so locals can't help but have a sweet spot for him. But such fame comes with a lot of attention. While you wait for a seat to become available on the wraparound benches beneath *David*, spend some time with Michelangelo's lesser-known sculptures along the adjoining Hall of Prisoners. This corridor is lined with unfinished statues that offer an insight into the artist's habitual approach to carving.

MUSEO DELL'OPERA DEL DUOMO

Map 1; Piazza del Duomo 9, Duomo; ///cold.runner.museum; www.duomo.firenze.it

It's tempting to simply snap a photo of the Duomo and move on, but this museum behind the cathedral is a testament to the immense work and passion that went into building it. At the entrance, the Corridoio dell'Opera is engraved with the names of some of the thousands of artisans, architects and humanists who contributed to the build, their work documented through multimedia displays or art they designed.

» **Don't leave without** seeing the original bronze doors of the Baptistery, designed after a competition for the commission in 1401, which many scholars define as the beginning of the Renaissance.

CAPPELLA BRANCACCI

Map 3; Santa Maria del Carmine, Piazza del Carmine 14 , Santo Spirito; ///runner.device.pounce; 055 276 8224

The Renaissance rears its head proudly in Florence, so it's easy to assume the roughly hewn Santa Maria del Carmine contains nothing of note. Found via a cloister, however, is what many call the "Sistine Chapel of the early Renaissance". Completed in part by Masolino, but more famously by Masaccio, the Brancacci Chapel's St Peter-themed fresco cycle was key for its development of spatial perspective and depth. It's magical to gaze upon, especially knowing that the frescoes were spared from a 1771 church fire – divine intervention, if you will.

Try it!
SCULPT A STATUE

Make like a Renaissance master and take a sculpture course at Galleria Romanelli (*www.raffaelloromanelli.com*), where you'll learn to model a clay sculpture, make a plaster cast or sculpt marble.

City History

The Renaissance may be Florence's calling card,
but it's only one part of the city's history. Tales
of famous families and creative minds abound,
and reaffirm why locals adore living here.

PALAZZO DAVANZATI

Map 1; Via Porta Rossa, Duomo; ///monday.strapped.howler;
www.bargellomusei.beniculturali.it

Florentines pride themselves on their heritage, the stories of their
ancestors woven into every brick of this city. Palazzo Davanzati, the
former home of an aristocratic family from the 14th century, is one
such relic of a life lived. The echoes of the past are felt everywhere
here, from the lavish living quarters that children darted through to
the cauldron-peppered kitchen where house staff toiled.

MUSEO SALVATORE FERRAGAMO

Map 1; Piazza di Santa Trinita 5r, Duomo; ///disposal.surveyed.arming;
www.ferragamo.commuseo

He might have been the "shoemaker to the stars" in the 1920s but
Salvatore Ferragamo had humble beginnings in Campania. He's
held up as a Florentine, though, with the Palazzo Spini Feroni

housing his original boutique and museum. Exhibitions often explore his ties to the US, silver screen shoemaking and experimentation with innovative materials like fish skin. Given how much a well-made shoe is worshipped in Florence, this museum just fits.

MUSEO DEGLI INNOCENTI

Map 4; Piazza della Santissima Annunziata 13, San Marco; ///manuals.wept.spades; www.museodeglinnocenti.it

Europe's first secular orphanage, the 15th-century Ospedale degli Innocenti is a monument to Florentine humanism. Here, orphaned or abandoned children were left at the entrance to be cared for by nurses, some with identifying objects from parents who planned to return. A poignant exhibit, made up of tiny drawers dedicated to each child, displays these lockets and rosaries, and leaves a lasting impression.

>> **Don't leave without** checking out the impressive art collection, which includes the *Adoration of the Magi* by Ghirlandaio.

LA SINAGOGA DEL FIRENZE

Map 2; Via Luigi Carlo Farini 6, Sant'Ambrogio; ///restrict.rattler.pockets; www.firenzebraica.it

For three centuries, Florence's Jewish community was confined to a ghetto in the city centre. Upon gaining citizenship in the mid-1800s, Jewish people decided to build a synagogue. Photographs and ornaments in the synagogue's museum honour the resilient locals, who today come together during the Balagan Cafè series on summer nights, when kosher food and klezmer music takes over the gardens.

CASA DI DANTE

Map 1; Via Santa Margherita 1, Duomo; ///remarks.outright.endings;
www.museocasadidante.it

Florentine poet Dante certainly rivals *David* as the poster boy for the city. After all, his bold choice to write *Divine Comedy* in the spoken vernacular instead of Latin helped establish the standardized Italian language spoken today. This house-museum anchors you in the beloved local's life, shining a light on his writing process and painful exile from the city he called home. Respect his legacy (and avoid eye rolls from the locals) by learning the language basics for your visit.

GUCCI GARDEN

Map 1; Piazza della Signoria 10, Duomo; ///coveted.deaf.thinkers;
www.guccigarden.gucci.com

People often associate Via Tornabuoni with high fashion, but most of the names lining the luxury drag aren't exactly local. The Gucci house, however, is as Florentine as it gets: the story began with Guccio Gucci opening a leather goods shop on Via della Vigna Nuova in 1921.

Shh!

Collecting is a Florentine pastime, and the 19th-century master of the hobby was Frederick Stibbert. Discover his collection, which includes spears and rugs, at Museo Stibbert *(www.museostibbert.it)*. The hours can be sporadic, with the odd DJ set or market thrown in, so check the website.

The Gucci Garden's rotating exhibitions pay tribute to the brand's major campaigns under current creative director Alessandro Michele, but also nod to its history and love for florals in the Gucci Bloom Room.

» **Don't leave without** visiting the boutique for merchandise exclusive to the Garden, and the Gucci Osteria for lunch.

PALAZZO VECCHIO

Map 1; Piazza della Signoria, Duomo; ///making.swan.clan; 055 276 8325

Secret passageways where the Medici stowed treasures, remains of a Roman amphitheatre underground, a role in the film *Inferno*: it's safe to say that the Palazzo Vecchio is unlike any other town hall in the world. As Florence's seat of civic power, it's still the spot where locals might go to resolve a bureaucratic issue, tie the knot in a civil ceremony or admire the city from its imposing tower *(p179)*.

BASILICA DI SANTA CROCE

Map 2; Piazza di Santa Croce 16, Santa Croce;
///trimmer.pipeline.trainer; www.santacroceopera.it

Stendhal Syndrome originated in this very basilica, where the likes of Galileo and Michelangelo are buried. This psychosomatic condition of hallucinations and dizziness is said to afflict sensitive souls who are exposed to overwhelmingly beautiful art – say, Giotto's fresco cycle in the Peruzzi chapel, or the perfect proportions of the former chapter house. The term came from the French author Stendhal, whose 19th-century travel writings detailed the flood of emotions he experienced in this divine complex. Prepare to swoon.

Contemporary Art

Florence is no Berlin, as the locals will point out with a mix of pride and sheepishness, but the modern art scene is picking up new steam thanks to forward-thinking gallerists and young artists with a dream.

STREET LEVELS GALLERY

Map 4; Via Palazzuolo 74, Santa Maria Novella; ///knots.silk.crimson; www.streetlevelsgallery.com

It can be heart-palpitating to think about graffiti plastered over Florence's historic buildings, but Street Levels Gallery was born to question art's role in this great city. Florence's first space dedicated to urban artwork champions local artists like Clet, who's known for plastering stickers on the city's street signs (and infuriating the

Try it!
GET CREATIVE

If Florence's budding artists have inspired your own creative impulses, check out MAD – Murate Art District *(www.murateartdistrict.it)* where craft workshops are held in a former jail.

council). Art students converge at the private viewings, queuing for red wine served up by heavily pierced staff and debating the latest artist to grace the exposed brick walls.

MANIFATTURA TABACCHI

Map 6; Via delle Cascine 35, Novoli; ///estimate.hairpin.stack; www.manifatturatabacchi.com

A former tobacco factory, this multi-functional space is where students from nearby UniFi get inspired to produce forward-thinking projects. NAM – Not a Museum, the site's contemporary art programme – encourages a rethinking of the world, whether it's through films that address gender identity or installations that ponder the climate crisis.

» Don't leave without breaking for brunch at the on-site Bulli & Balene restaurant, if you're visiting at the weekend.

SRISA GALLERY

Map 4; Via San Gallo 53r, San Marco; ///dawn.rotation.helm; www.srisa.gallery

Florence might be a revolving door of art students, but some end up settling here and leaving their mark. Helping them do so is artist Rebecca Olsen, whose parents founded Santa Reparata International School of Art (SRISA). As well as running the school, Rebecca co-curates the non-profit gallery, which hosts shows by students, faculty and alumni. The joy of being here comes from breathing in the youthful, international energy and digesting new work produced on the ground in Florence, rather than brought in from afar.

FORTE DI BELVEDERE

Map 5; Via di San Leonardo 1, San Niccolò; ///pebble.revise.riper; www.cultura.comune.fi.it

When Kim Kardashian wed Kanye West here in 2014, it stirred up grumbles from the locals, but nonetheless catapulted the long-closed Medici fort back into public consciousness. Now, visiting the former stronghold has become a summer ritual, when contemporary sculptures are peppered throughout the sprawling, hilltop grounds.

EDUARDO SECCI FIRENZE

Map 4; Piazza Carlo Goldoni 2, Santa Maria Novella; ///ribs.avoiding.panics; www.eduardosecci.com

Suits and cocktail dresses wafting through Piazza Carlo Goldoni are a sure sign that there's a new show on at the Secci. Namesake Eduardo was Italy's youngest gallerist when he entered the art world at 19, and his monographic exhibitions fittingly spotlight emerging and mid-career artists from Italy and beyond. Coveted opening nights are invite-only for the Italian glitterati, after which those with an interest in in-your-face brushwork are welcome.

MUSEO NOVECENTO

Map 4; Piazza di Santa Maria Novella 10, Santa Maria Novella; ///urban.proper.sweated; www.museonovecento.it

After the Arno flood of 1966 destroyed much of Florence's art, historian Carlo Ludovico Ragghianti took it upon himself to re-establish the city's artistic heft. He called on international artists to donate works to the city, and over 280 responded with 20th-century art. In 2014, the pieces were gathered in one place for the first time: the Museo Novecento. Beyond this moving permanent collection, film screenings and concerts are frequently held in tandem with colourful exhibitions.

PALAZZO STROZZI

Map 1; Piazza degli Strozzi, Duomo; ///pictures.fries.racing; www.palazzostrozzi.org

A Renaissance palace exhibiting modern art might seem sacrilegious, but Palazzo Strozzi encapsulates the essence of Florence: respecting the old while welcoming the new. Here, that means avant-garde exhibits like two giant tunnel slides in the inner courtyard. On Thursday evenings, friends take over said courtyard with drinks before heading to La Strozzina – the gallery in the palace's former cellar – for events.

» Don't leave without enjoying bubbles and gourmet finger food at the stylish café before scouring the bookshop for design souvenirs.

ARIA ART GALLERY

Map 1; Borgo Santi Apostoli 40, Duomo; ///jogging.rescue.sticking; www.ariaartgallery.com

Aria first opened its renowned doors in Pietrasanta, a Tuscan town known for mosaics, marble and bronze. This theme – fine materials, sinuous sculptures – endured through the gallery's relocation to Florence, though installations and holograms appear just as often. Essentially, the collection consists of whatever impresses artistic director Antonio Budetta, which is usually experimental or bold art.

On Stage and Screen

The performing arts have been a beloved pastime since the days when pageantries were put on for the Medici. Today, locals still pass hours in sumptuous buildings, entertained by theatre and cinema.

ST MARK'S ENGLISH CHURCH

Map 3; Via Maggio 16, Santo Spirito; ///bicker.vibrate.phones; www.stmarksitaly.com

Many of Italy's churches are wholly dedicated to worship, so St Mark's stands out with its rich cultural programme. Welcoming anyone and everyone are the iconic opera nights, where the arias of Verdi, Puccini and Rossini echoing below a stencilled pre-Raphaelite ceiling is as goosebump-inducing as it gets. Fawn over the acoustics with the wider community at the informal *aperitivo* that follows every performance.

TEATRO DELLA PERGOLA

Map 2; Via della Pergola 12/32, Duomo; ///disputes.will.bonnet; www.teatrodellapergola.com

Opera originated in Florence in the 15th century, and it wasn't long before a grand theatre was constructed for the court to enjoy a good show. Many rich families contributed to the build and, in

Book the Pergola Grand Tour – running on selected dates – to see the sumptuous interior up close and go backstage.

return, would enjoy performances from the plush box seats. When watching a chamber music or opera show here, look up: wooden coats of arms on these boxes signal the families who came before you.

CINEMA ODEON

Map 1; Piazza degli Strozzi 2r, Duomo; ///helping.farm.gifts; www.odeonfirenze.com

In a Renaissance-heavy city, it's easy to forget that the roaring twenties made a mark here. A 1920s magic remains at this century-strong opulent theatre, where movie-goers settle into gold velvet chairs for arty flicks or blockbusters in their original language (mostly English). When the film suddenly stops and the lights turn on, don't panic: it's simply the old-school interval and a signal to refill your popcorn.

» Don't leave without seeing what events are on: the cinema hosts festivals and 1920s-inspired parties on occasion.

CINEMA IN VILLA AT VILLA BARDINI

Map 5; Costa San Giorgio 2, San Niccolò; ///claps.ruffle.racks; www.villabardini.it

On balmy nights, Florentines don their comfy shoes for an uphill walk to Villa Bardini to enjoy the open-air theatre, only set up in the summer months. Surrounded by picturesque gardens and the city glittering below you, you'll continually be distracted from what's playing on the big screen, but the film is hardly the reason you came.

TEATRO NICCOLINI

Map 1; Via Ricasoli 3, Duomo; ///farmed.renting.arrived;
www.teatroniccolini.com

Ever since its inauguration in the 17th century, Niccolini has been captivating audiences with great theatre. The programme, managed by the Teatro della Pergola, focuses on niche plays like a dramatization of a Samuel Beckett short story or a re-enactment of Machiavelli's life.

» Don't leave without visiting the in-house bar for a casual *aperitivo* (you can't go wrong ordering a spritz) before a show.

TEATRO VERDI

Map 2; Via Ghibellina 99, Santa Croce; ///clashes.removes.tigers;
www.teatroverdifirenze.it

Traditional and contemporary arts live in perfect harmony at this 19th-century theatre. It's a home for the Orchestra della Toscana, considered one of Italy's best orchestras. And it's also a stage for theatre productions, dance shows, musicals and pop concerts.

CINEMA LA COMPAGNIA

Map 4; Via Camillo Cavour 50r, San Lorenzo; ///deeper.hilltop.toolbar;
www.cinemalacompagnia.it

Cinephiles hold this cinema in high regard. Beyond the documentary screenings, the festivals hosted here are a chance to bask in the brilliance of film-makers, like South Korea's famed artists during the Florence Korea Film Fest, or those telling underrepresented stories at the Florence Queer Festival.

Liked by the locals

"For over twenty years, the Florence Korea Film Fest has been building an ideological yet solid bridge between two countries in a celebration of cultural dialogue and the big screen."

RICCARDO GELLI, DIRECTOR OF THE
FLORENCE KOREA FILM FEST

Get Crafty

*People flock to Florence in the hope of joining
the ranks of artisans who breathe life into the city.
Though such skills don't come easy, it's fun trying to
master pottery or marbling at expert-led workshops.*

PAPER MARBLING WITH RICCARDO LUCI

Map 4; Via del Parione 35r, Santa Maria Novella;
///cycle.sponsors.tapers; www.riccardoluci.com

Marbled paper is an art form that Florence – and Riccardo Luci –
hold dear. Riccardo proudly comes from four generations of
bookmakers, and he keeps the tradition alive at his paint-splattered
studio; come to watch him swirl bright dyes across a tray of liquid
before dipping the paper in. Have a play yourself and return the
next day to pick up your dried masterpiece.

LEATHER-MAKING WORKSHOP

Map 2; Borgo Santa Croce 17, Santa Croce; ///monopoly.rising.entire;
info@florencefashiontour.com

To understand the detail that goes into every leather good made in
Florence, you need to smell, feel, cut and stitch it yourself. Chic young
Florentine Alice Cozzi has channelled her *haute couture* expertise

into a hands-on workshop for this purpose, introducing you to an artisan who you'll spend an afternoon with. While you craft a belt, keyring or coin purse, you'll learn how to recognize quality leather and what phrases like "split grain" and "top grain" mean.

JEWELLERY MAKING AT LINFA STUDIO GALLERY

Map 2; Borgo Allegri 60r, Santa Croce; ///magma.surging.crest; www.linfastudiogallery.com

This light and airy studio gallery is liveliest when filled with "weekend goldsmiths" taking on the Basic Metalsmithing course. Easy-going jeweller Valentina Caprini guides you through cutting, hammering and soldering, sending you home with your own labour of love (most often in the form of a brass ring). Coffee breaks and banter are part of the process, and will have you feeling like a proper metalsmith.

» Don't leave without poking your head into the secret garden at the back of the studio space for some fresh air.

The Charles Cecil Studios (*www.charlescecilstudios.com*) in San Frediano is brilliant for full-time painting courses. Unbeknown to non-students, though, are the Thursday evening events, when members of the public are unofficially invited to come along to free art history lectures. Listen to Charles talk about Titian before mingling over wine.

Solo, Pair, Crowd

Though not everyone has what it takes to become an artisan, Florence welcomes anyone willing to try.

FLYING SOLO

Paint with passion

Explore the principles of oil painting without the pressure of long-term art school at The Florence Studio in the Duomo area. Canadians Frank and Laura will introduce you to techniques in a three-hour workshop.

IN A PAIR

Swap souvenirs

Bring your date to Officina Nora in Santo Spirito and craft one another a unique pendant. On the Souvenir Workshop, you'll learn about the properties of metal and how to use it.

FOR A CROWD

Play with clay

Enjoy a birthday with a difference at Mud Pottery Club in Le Cure, gathering your friends on one of the big tables and letting your creativity run wild with the clay. It's always fun to see what everyone crafts.

OFFICINA LABORATORIO CERAMICA

Map 6; Via Nardo di Cione 6, Sant'Ambrogio; ///tablets.employ.shoppers; 339 131 2990

One of the joys of hosting a dinner party is showing off your finest ceramics, especially when you can say you decorated them in Florence. Book onto a workshop at "OffLab" to do just that, painting already sculpted plates alongside friends.

POTTERY AT BOTTEGA PENDOLARE

Map 2; Via degli Alfani 33r, Sant'Ambrogio; ///croak.huddled.both; 333 134 4381

Jaded by painting watercolours along the Arno, many Florentines are turning to pottery to channel their artistic energy. In this former bike shop, artist Violet will have you throwing your own pots before she glazes and fires them. She can post them home to you if you ask nicely.

» Don't leave without buying one of Violet's hand-thrown nude pots or vases for a unique piece from the city's new wave of ceramicists.

LA SERRA M.K. TEXTILE ATELIER

Map 4; Via Salvestrina 1, San Marco; ///homes.waffle.embarks; www.mktextileatelier.com

In Italy, nonna's hand-knitted hand-me-downs are heirlooms. Make your own piece to pass on to future generations in this converted greenhouse, where textile designers Karl and Margherita teach you how to decorate a tote bag, place mat or table runner using silkscreen, stencilling, block-printing or hand-painting techniques.

A day of
literary history

Countless writers have been influenced by Florence and left their mark here, from medieval master Dante to Renaissance author Niccolò Machiavelli. Among those who became smitten with the city's painterly sunsets and breezy lifestyle were many 19th-century Brits, including poets Elizabeth Barrett and Robert Browning and *A Room With a View* author E M Forster. Breathe in the literary legacy through these streets – perhaps you'll also be inspired to put pen to paper.

Uncover British roots at
HAROLD ACTON
LIBRARY
Traces of a British literary community remain at this library in the British Institute of Florence. Get a one-day membership and see if there are any talks on, or enjoy the stunning view from the windows.

SANTO SPIRITO

Get acquainted at
CASA GUIDI
The Brownings lived here for about 15 years, with Elizabeth house-bound with spinal disease for a long time. Get a sense of what her view of the city was like from here.

1. Casa Guidi
Piazza San Felice 8, Santo Spirito; 347 696 8528
///length.prongs.tallest

2. Harold Acton Library
British Institute of Florence, Lungarno Guicciardini 9, Santo Spirito; www.british institute.it
///sifts.thus.polite

3. Giubbe Rosse
Piazza della Repubblica 13/14r, Duomo; 055 212 280
///sour.remotes.cats

4. Casa di Dante
Via Santa Margherita 1, Duomo; www.museocasa didante.it
///raking.image.silk

5. Basilica di Santa Croce
Piazza di Santa Croce 16, Santa Croce; www.santa croceopera.it
///trimmer.pipeline.trainer

📍 **Piazza de' Pitti 37**
///hopes.surfed.grab

📍 **Badia Fiorentina**
///fooling.swaps.voter

Settle in at
GIUBBE ROSSE

Nibble on snacks at this historic café, where creatives would come to write during the Futurist movement of the early 20th century.

3

VIA DEL CORSO

DUOMO

Pop into
CASA DI DANTE

Explore the artifacts at this museum, which pays tribute to the *Somma Poeta* ("Supreme Poet") and father of the Italian language. It's believed that Dante was born around this spot.

4

Badia Fiorentina *monastery is where Dante first set eyes upon his great love Beatrice, and where the bells ring out in* Paradiso XV.

5

Immerse yourself at the
BASILICA DI SANTA CROCE

Get meta at the burial site of Ugo Foscolo, the author of *Dei Sepolcri*, a poetic response to a Napoleonic ruling regulating the size and grandeur of tombs.

Though Fyodor Dostoevsky had disdain for the city and its tourists, he chose to work on The Idiot *from* **Piazza de' Pitti 37**.

SAN LORENZO

SAN MARCO

PIAZZA DI SAN LORENZO

VIA DEI SERVI

PIAZZA SAN GIOVANNI

PIAZZA DEL DUOMO

NTA RIA VELLA

VIA DE TORNABUONI

PELLICCERIA

VIA PORTA ROSSA

Ponte S. Trinita

Arno

ORGO SAN IACOPO

Ponte Vecchio

VIA DEL PROCONSOLO

VIA DELL'ANGUILLARA

VIA GIUSEPPE VERDI

SANTA CROCE

PIAZZA DI SANTA CROCE

LUNGARNO TORRIGIANI

SAN NICCOLÒ

Giardino Bardini

Giardino di Boboli

0 metres		250
0 yards		250

NIGHTLIFE

Is there anything more delightful than a Florentine evening? Lingering over drinks, swaying to live music and socializing in piazzas – truly perfetto.

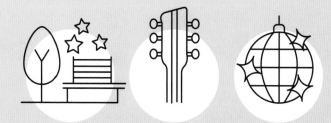

Aperitivo Spots

A practice central to Italian social lives, aperitivo is the golden hour that sets you up for the night. With work over and dinner not for a few hours, friends gather for a drink and complimentary snacks.

NOVE7

Map 2; Borgo la Croce 97r, Sant'Ambrogio; ///hydrant.escapes.cliff; 340 618 7933

Nove7 has an unspoken dress code of black leather jackets, boots and blue jeans. Get it wrong and you'll stand out among the cool Italian students who linger over a Campari spritz as they smoke and gossip; get it right and you'll be welcomed into the fold. The only thing better than their nod of approval is the divine plate of mini pizzas, fried doughballs and truffle croquettes thrown in with the €5 cocktails.

PROCACCI

Map 1; Via de' Tornabuoni 64r, Duomo; ///bicker.olive.painting; www.procacci1885.it

Sprezzatura – that distinctly Italian, devil-may-care elegance – is always in the air at this Art Deco bar, where old-timers in fur coats watch the world go by and men in just-shined shoes lean over the tabletops outside. A glass of champagne and a truffle brioche bun here make for a wonderful start to the night – just remember to forgo the trainers and T-shirt in favour of something smarter (you'll encounter some serious side-eye if you don't).

» **Don't leave without** buying some gourmet gifts from the shop to take back home, like jarred truffle butter and artisan chocolate.

BUCA10

Map 2; Via Fiesolana 10, Sant'Ambrogio; ///siesta.inherit.prepared; www.buca10.it

This warm and welcoming hole in the wall (which is pretty much what *buca* translates as) serves *aperitivo* with a difference: sweet or savoury snacks to suit whichever wine or cocktail you order. Go for a fruity red, and the staff might bring you chocolate or orange-zest *cantucci*; a fresh white and you'll get rosemary and sea salt *taralli* or some cured hams and cheeses. Expect groups of friends enjoying some low-key respite on a rainy evening, engrossed in a game of cards or plucking a few tunes on a guitar while sipping their wine.

TABACCHI NUVOLA

Map 3; Piazza del Carmine, San Frediano; ///cool.dragons.races

Tabacchi Nuvola may not be anything fancy, but that's sort of the point. The atmosphere is studenty and rowdy but decidedly Italian. Come for the cheap and strong cocktails (the negronis are particularly potent), stay for the great snacks and a lovely corner spot in Piazza del Carmine.

SOUL KITCHEN

Map 2; Via dei Benci 34r, Santa Croce; ///offshore.normal.warrior;
www.soulkitchenfirenze.it

Santa Croce's reputation as one of Florence's liveliest areas could well be down to Soul Kitchen. From 7pm, high energy reverberates off the exposed brick walls here as friends enjoy *aperecina* (a blend of *aperitivo* and dinner) for just €10. And the fun doesn't stop once *aperitivo* is over. People stay put to chat with the bartenders, sip movie-inspired cocktails and get dancing to DJ sets.

BULLI E BALENE

Map 3; Via dello Sprone 14r, Santo Spirito; ///defining.herbs.panther;
055 205 2252

The *aperitivo* drink of choice for many Florentines is a spritz, a mix of prosecco and bitters, and an acquired taste. Near enough every bar in the city makes a mean variation, but this Venetian-inspired spot thinks beyond Aperol and Campari for its bitters with the likes

Hidden in a courtyard off Florence's shopping street, Via dei Calzaiuoli, Serre Torrigiani in Piazzetta *(Piazza dei Tre Re 1)* is a place of refuge for tired locals. This unexpected oasis is the place to relax over a cooling mint and elderflower drink and a slice of slow-rise *pinsa* (the precursor to pizza). Check online for summer events, which include tarot reading and yoga.

of Venetian standby Select or the artichoke-infused Cynar. It also trades out Tuscan *taglieri* (meat and cheese boards) for Venetian-style *cicchetti* (goodies like whipped codfish served on toast). Savour it all in the little outdoor seating nook while watching the world go by.

PASTICCERIA DEANNA

Map 4; Piazza della Stazione 54, Santa Maria Novella; ///ember.betrayal.cover; www.pasticceriadeanna.it

If anything gives middle-aged Florentines a hit of nostalgia, it's the phrase *"ci vediamo al Deanna"* ("see you at Deanna!"): four simple words that ensured a friend would be waiting by the window of this café. Decades after opening, Deanna remains a beloved meeting point for both long-timers and a younger generation of locals. Girlfriends drop in for a coffee and a *cornetto* before work, promising to return when the day is done for a casual *aperitivo* and a natter about trivial office politics.

» Don't leave without ordering a Crodino – a soft drink prepared with oranges, herbal extracts and (lots of) sugar.

MOSTODOLCE

Map 4; Via Nazionale 114r, San Lorenzo; ///foiled.ranked.copiers; www.mostodolce.it

Italian geezers watch the football on big screens here, tucking into deep-fried snacks as they lament a missed goal. Order Martellina – a local chestnut honey beer – and settle in for an evening of rowdy chatter, rock music and football commentary.

Open-Air Hangouts

This may be Italy, but Florence isn't balmy all year. Warm summer nights are cherished with abandon, and see the streets, piazzas and riversides come alive with friends and families enjoying time outdoors.

PIAZZA SANTO SPIRITO

Map 3; Santo Spirito; ///eyebrows.forced.swear

When Florentines think of their city on a summer weekend, it's likely their minds will drift to this lively little piazza. From mid-afternoon onwards, a laidback community of artists and musicians flood into the square – some cradling an Aperol Spritz on alfresco restaurant tables, others mingling under the shadow of the 15th-century basilica. It's the perfect place to make new friends, practising your Italian with gap year students and middle-aged hippies.

RIVER URBAN BEACH

Map 5; Piazza Giuseppe Poggi, San Niccolò; ///spacing.backs.neater; www.riverurbanbeach.it

Florence might not have the dreamy coastlines of southern Italy, but the palm trees and sand at this pop-up beach along the banks of the Arno are enough to fool you. It's easy to lose the afternoon playing a

Don't follow the foolhardy who strip off before getting in the Arno to cool down – there are fresh showers for that.

bout of volleyball, unwinding under frilly parasols and tucking into street food from a handful of vendors. Before you know it, it's evening, and DJs are blasting out pop tunes while you order cocktails.

HABANA 500
Map 6; Lungarno Guglielmo Pecori Giraldi, Ponte San Niccolò, Santa Croce; ///spill.limbs.amuses; www.habana500firenze.it

As the city gears up for alfresco revelry in late spring, Habana 500 is always one of the first places to open its doors. This cocktail bar along the Arno brings a slice of Cuba to Florence, with fresh mojitos mixed at the bar, salsa dancers entertaining on wooden decking and a live band providing percussion rhythms. Soak up the easy-going vibes while relaxing on a vintage deckchair, the sun setting over the river.

PIAZZA SANT'AMBROGIO
Map 2; Sant'Ambrogio; ///slipping.swear.spooned

It might be central, but Sant'Ambrogio has a village-like air; residents pass days haggling at the historic market or catching up on a park bench. This casual and decidedly local nature extends to the nightlife scene, the heart of which is this piazza and its surrounding cheap bars. Mates meet here when evening approaches, happy to bask in the relaxed atmosphere and see where the night takes them.

» **Don't leave without** moving onto Borgo la Croce, a street filled with bars and restaurants – perfect for an impromptu spritz crawl.

Solo, Pair, Crowd

Florence's open-air spots welcome everyone with, well, open arms. Party under the stars or let the night pass lingering on a terrace.

FLYING SOLO
A breezy evening
Order a beer from the Il Tempio kiosk and find a table to perch at, sipping your drink while gazing out across the river. Set in the Caponnetto Gardens, it's a perfectly quiet and chilled spot to wind down in.

IN A PAIR
Dinner date
Nurse a bottle of wine and a platter of bruschetta at Santarosa Bistrot, a picturesque patio with tables dotted around a romantic rose garden in San Frediano.

FOR A CROWD
Have some Pride
Pride Park NCS, Florence's historic LGBTQ+ event, brings the party to public parks in June. Gather your gang and rainbow flags and party into the balmy night with other revellers.

GIARDINO DELLA FORTEZZA

Map 4; enter at Viale Filippo Strozzi, Santa Maria Novella;
///dressing.vivid.packing

If anything makes the hot, dry summer nights unbearable, it's the mass crowds congregating in the city centre. Those who can't stand the excess body heat drift out to the large lake at Fortezza, a park just outside the city walls that surprisingly few people seem to know exists. Cacophonous voices hang in the breezy air here, be it the joyful cheers while football matches are livestreamed, the live music drifting from festival-style stages or the gasps of satisfaction after tucking in to street food stall offerings. Come at sunset, bring a blanket to lounge on and savour the summer.

» Don't leave without enjoying a Sex on the Beach at OFF Bar, the main drinking spot here. It avoids only serving spritz on repeat with a menu of funky drinks and Thai food.

MOLO 5 FIRENZE

Map 6; Lungarno Cristoforo Colombo, Campo di Marte;
///absorbs.oiled.nozzle

Of all the Arno spots that come into their own in the summer, Molo 5 Firenze is the perfect tonic after a long day. Festival vibes prevail, with mellow tunes and the tantalizing smell of street food tempting people like a beacon. The changeable food vendors are iconic Florentine restaurants in pop-up form, so you won't miss out on your favourite organic pizza from SimBIOsi or fish tacos from Pescepane simply because you can't bear to sit inside a hot restaurant. Eat your chosen treat on the banks, your legs dangling a few metres from the water.

Live Music

The creativity that flows through Florence isn't limited to jewellers and sculptors. Beyond the guitarist strumming in the piazza are musicians who soundtrack evenings in quaint venues.

JAZZ CLUB FIRENZE

Map 2; Via Nuova dei Caccini 3, Sant'Ambrogio; ///coherent.suckle.picture

If there was ever a musical style to complement Florence's easy-going nature, it would be jazz. This intimate bar has been accompanying laidback nights out since 1979, with established and emerging artists playing jazz, blues, funk and, unexpectedly, rock tunes. Expect young musicians chatting around candlelit tables, praising the soft thud of a double bass during a jam session.

LE MURATE CAFFÈ LETTERARIO

Map 2; Piazza delle Murate, Santa Croce; ///opponent.angle.lime; www.lemurate.it

Visit this former prison turned literary café by day and you'll join budding poets sinking into a couch, engrossed by a page turner as they cradle a coffee. At sunset, everyone heads out into the courtyard with a glass of vino, seduced by jazz, classical and rock performances.

IL CONVENTINO CAFFÉ LETTERARIO
Map 3; Via Giano della Bella 20, San Frediano; ///passing.splice.spare;
www.ilconventinofirenze.it

Creatives pass days peacefully here, playing chess, practising Italian
and awaiting sweet melodies to fill the courtyard. On Thursday, it'll
be classical music courtesy of the Fiesole Music School and the
Conservatory; on Sunday, local jazz bands lift *aperitivo* hour.
» Don't leave without taking a crochet lesson or a marbled paper
workshop at this former cloister turned multifunctional space.

OSTELLO TASSO
Map 3; Via Villani 15, Piazza Tasso, San Frediano;
///tanks.trams.going; 055 060 2087

There's a hint of school disco vibes at this hostel bar (well, it used
to be a school), but with the added bonus of a buzzing bar serving
up cocktails. Set in the old assembly hall, Tasso sees hostel guests
trying their luck at Wednesday open mic nights and swing bands
impressing in-the-know locals.

Try it!
RECORD A TUNE

If Florence's musical talent has inspired you
to write your own masterpiece, head to
Manifattura Tabacchi *(www.manifattura
tabacchi.com)* and track it at LoudLift, the
first self-operated recording booth in Italy.

NOF

Map 3; Borgo San Frediano 17/19r, San Frediano;
///seasons.stage.coverage; www.nofclub.it

Even if you fail to squeeze into this tiny free venue, the good vibes are palpable from the street, where a huge window behind the small stage lets you see the bands playing. Of course, the music (usually alternative sounds) is best heard inside, so best to turn up early.

CIRCOLO AURORA FIRENZE

Map 3; Piazza Torquato Tasso 1, Santo Spirito; ///people.carpets.struck;
055 224 059

Originally anti-fascist gathering points for lively debates and political rallies, Florence's Circoli Arci are a dying breed today. The few that do remain are more like blue-collar social clubs where all manner of events unfold. This ivy-clad cottage, built into the old city walls, is one such surviving stronghold, where regulars sit and chat while enjoying Cuban jazz and acoustic guitar in a casual environment.

INSTABILE – CULTURE IN MOVIMENTO

Map 6; Via della Funda 20, Varlungo; ///store.shifting.saucepan

Built on a patch of riverbank under a motorway bridge, this alfresco venue has the air of an underground festival. It's delightfully different from the rest of the city, festooned with fairy lights under which crowds sway to Balkan jazz, folk and orchestral music.

» Don't leave without getting your tarot read by the nomadic fortune teller who often sets up shop here in the evenings.

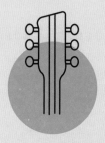

Liked by the locals

"Florence has much more than mainstream clubbing if you go out of the centre. There's something different every weekend at local places like Instabile – Balkan music concerts, traditional folk concerts and workshops."

LAYLA DARI, ITALIAN TEACHER WITH A PHD
IN HISTORY OF ART AND PERFORMING ARTS

Dance Spots

Banish any preconceived ideas of a city that never gets wild. Clubbing might be a happy afterthought as opposed to a main event, but Florentines know how to party when a decadent club comes calling.

TENAX

Map 6; Via Pratese 46, Peretola; ///loans.kinks.dodging; www.tenax.org

You might not expect to find this debauched underground club in genteel Florence, but that's exactly why it's needed. Tenax has been somewhere for Florentines to let loose to new sounds since 1981, opening when new wave and punk music were at their peak. Though it's moved beyond its indie origins today, with DJs thumping out everything from reggaeton to techno, Tenax remains an iconic place to both lose and find yourself under the strobe lights.

QUEER

Map 2; Borgo Allegri 9r, Santa Croce; ///stiff.translate.rooms; 366 275 9210

At the entrance to this intimate spot, neon lights illuminate a simple, powerful word: Queer. New friends chat like old chums inside this welcoming LGBTQ+ haven, nursing a cocktail (likely named after

Shirley Temple) while Britney's *Baby One More Time* blasts through the speakers. Even if you've turned up alone, it won't be long before you're hands-in-the-air boogying to pop classics on the teeny dance floor – if the friendly regulars have anything to do with it.

» **Don't leave without** chatting to owner Andrea at the bar, who will likely advise you on the best cocktail to order.

YAB

Map 1; Via dei Sassetti 5r, Duomo; ///update.instant.lifted; www.yab.it

Ask a middle-aged Florentine if they've ever been to YAB and watch their eyes twinkle as they recount the time they may or may not have seen Madonna dancing with Yves Saint Laurent there. The city's most famous *discoteca* has been on the scene since most care to remember (1979), and new generations are still having nights to fill their memoirs with here. The drinks are strong, the music is loud and the endless challenge of trying to make it past the backstage area and downstairs to the more exclusive dance floor is always fun.

Shh!

Though LGBTQ+ club Fabrik Firenze *(www.fabrikfirenze.it)* on Florence's outskirts is reserved for members, there's still a way to indulge in the disco music and themed nights if you're only passing through town. Purchase a "Travel" subscription – it gives you access to all the clubs in Italy part of the ARCO network, which promotes the creation of safe, inclusive spaces and clubs.

BLANCO BEACH BAR

Map 6; Viale Generale dalla Chiesa 11, Campo di Marte;
///live.faster.crowbar; www.blancobeachbar.it

Summer officially starts for Florence's glamour squad when upmarket nightclub Otel opens its pop-up beach club. The guests switch out their double leather for black dresses and linen shirts, ready to linger under white parasols and rate each other's outfits. It's the place to be on a balmy Thursday night, when crowds dance to hip-hop, reggaeton and Latin pop while palm trees sway.

CLUB 21

Map 1; Via dei Cimatori 13r, Duomo; ///curry.tanked.dominate;
www.club21florence.com

Club 21 is every Polimoda fashion student's favourite place to party, especially at the big events held here during Pitti Uomo (p9). The rest of the year, it's Thursday's Tropical Animals student night that draws them in, whether they've got a stint DJing behind the decks or they're vibing to experimental techno on the dance floor.

THE LODGE

Map 5; Viale Giuseppe Poggi 1, San Niccolò; ///cobble.area.director;
www.thelodgeclub.com

Perched on a hill, The Lodge starts the evening as a bouji *aperitivo* spot – the kind of place where magnums of Moet are casually ordered to the table – before morphing into a pumping open-air club. Everyone seems to have a friend who knows the owners, but no

For another chic club with vast views, head to Flo Lounge Bar. Party until 4am before watching the sunrise.

one can get in after 11pm, so arrive early. Once you're in, the real magic is looking out across the glittering city below while you dance to classic club tunes.

VILLA VITTORIA

Map 4; Viale Filippo Strozzi 2, Fortezza, San Marco;
///dice.fact.fashion; www.villavittoriafirenze.com

Florentines love to hate this summer-only spot. Sure, there's a lot of champagne-spraying and people can get a bit messy (drinking too much is not the done thing in Florence), but it's without a doubt the city's most picturesque club. Dotting the grounds of an old villa are street food vans selling DIY *aperitivo,* cordoned-off VIP booths and myriad dance areas – plenty of space to escape corks popping.

» Don't leave without enjoying oysters and fried snacks from the Fishing Lab seafood van before getting your boogie on.

CRISCO CLUB

Map 2; Via Sant'Egidio 43r, Santa Croce;
///crisp.downward.tummy; www.criscoclub.com

Everything here pays homage to Manhattan's iconic gay club, the Crisco Disco. It's the signature red logo that draws men like a beacon, the black leather seats that mature bears flirt on and the kitschy strobe ball under which guys dance until the early hours (yep, this is a men's-only spot, with a cruising area to boot). Cheeky themed nights add a unique touch, like the underwear parties on Thursdays.

Late-Night Bites

If there's anything Florentines worship, it's food – no matter the hour. A bite after ambling through forgotten alleyways or clubbing in the outskirts is as customary as the aperitivo, if we may be so bold.

ACQUA AL 2

Map 1; Via della Vigna Vecchia 40r, Duomo;
///monkey.carpets.minute; 055 284 170

Acqua al 2 is one of the few trattorias that will welcome you in for a bowl of pasta even as the clocks are approaching midnight and most restaurants are shutting up shop. You'll be dining alongside a slightly more mature crowd of party-goers – you know, the kind who've drunk half a bottle of champagne at a gallery opening and don't fancy dancing all night.

FO'CACCIA LA NOTTE

Map 2; Via Giuseppe Verdi, 43, Santa Croce; ///stapled.drilling.remarks;
055 936 0449

You wouldn't be the first to spend Friday night mingling with new pals on Piazza Santa Croce, forgetting that you've not eaten since meeting those very friends during *apericena*. When hunger

strikes, follow the crowds migrating towards this "pizza window" – known as such because its counter faces directly onto the street – and get a filled focaccia to satisfy your grumbling stomach.
» Don't leave without ordering a slice of the signature pizza topped with pesto sauce, sun-dried tomatoes and parsley.

I'BANDITO
Map 6; Piazza Taddeo Gaddi, San Frediano; ///probably.graced.hidden; 327 066 5812

The passion with which locals talk about this 24-hour food truck will win you over before you even tuck into the food. In the queue behind you, students fresh from a night along the Oltrarno will likely tell you to order a juicy burger. Expect the sticklers for tradition to clapback sassily, instead insisting that you go for the *panino al lampredotto* – a Florentine classic, made from the fourth and final stomach of a cow. What will it be?

Shh!

Florence's secret bakeries have long been the charm of 4am street wandering. Being secret, though, the whereabouts are ever illusive – there one year, gone the next. Sniff out the smell of freshly baked croissants in the small hours, especially on the cobbled alleyways between Sant'Ambrogio and Santa Croce, and you might just spot a glint of light coming from behind a metal grate. Knock politely and see what happens.

Liked by the locals

"The clubbing scene can get pretty wild as a full-time DJ, but after a long night there's only one place the nightlife crew go for a freshly baked croissant and warm cappuccino before sunrise: I'Pappagallo."

NICCOLO MESSER, DJ, PRODUCER AND CO-FOUNDER OF FLORENCE AT NIGHT

I'PAPPAGALLO

Map 6; Via Fra' Giovanni Angelico 1r, Campo di Marte;
///full.smoker.soccer; 055 670 525

When the clubs close, DJs, promoters and bouncers migrate to this early-morning café. It might seem profane to order a cappuccino when you've not yet slept, but this party crew are convinced the milky coffee helps them sleep better. Expect a queue when the metal grate opens at 4am, just as dawn is breaking and the city's first workers are stirring.

LOS CHICOS

Map 1; Via dei Benci 15r, Santa Croce; ///verdict.finger.fooling; 055 051 0179

This late-night Tex Mex is an unlikely staple on a food scene where old-school Italian joints reign supreme. Yet, for the party-goers who stumble out of the nearby bars at 4am, hungrily scoffing tacos here is the best part of their night out.

IL FARAONE

Map 6; Via Bartolomeo Cristofori 14r, Romito; ///twitchy.courtyard.local;
055 366 592

Settling on the best kebab shop in town is a surprisingly contentious issue, but the voices that shout the loudest call for Il Faraone. It's a classic stop-off if you're taking a taxi home from Tenax *(p148)* and there's always a crowd outside, no doubt waiting for a flatbread stuffed with chips, pickles and juicy shredded chicken.

» Don't leave without ordering some almond baklava, drenched in honey and perfect for sweet cravings.

A classic night out in
Sant'Ambrogio

The Santa Croce area might get all the credit for having the city's best nightlife, but neighbouring Sant'Ambrogio is hot on its heels. This convivial patch of town has everything that makes a Florentine evening special: an iconic piazza perfect for people-watching, cosy restaurants serving up hearty food and dance floors to let loose on. Florentines rarely plan their nights to a strict schedule; instead, follow the laughter and chatter that fills these streets and see where the evening takes you.

1. MAD - Murate Art District
Piazza delle Murate;
www.murateartdistrict.it
///thrones.toward.closed

2. I Macci
Piazza Pietro Annigoni 3;
055 094 8777
///perfume.trusts.risky

3. Cibrèo
Via dei Macci 122r;
www.cibreo.com
///muddle.retrial.exposes

4. Piazza Sant'Ambrogio
///loudly.brush.paves

5. Rex Café
Via Fiesolana 25r;
www.rexfirenze.com
///patch.clubs.feathers

📍 **Bitter Bar**
///alert.freezing.slide

📍 **Alla Sosta dei Papi**
///observe.bridge.informs

Have a dance at 5
REX CAFÉ
This funky, packed bar is a defining part of Florentine nightlife. Dance to DJ sets blasting lounge, electro and a lot of house music into the early hours.

Bitter Bar *is known for experimenting with unusual bitters, getting customers to rethink what they know about cocktails.*

VIA FIESOL...

VIA DEI PEPI

VIA DEI PEPI

SANTA CROCE

VIA DI SAN GIUSEPPE

PIAZZA
MASSIMO
D'AZEGLIO

0 metres   100
0 yards   100

VIA DEI PILASTRI

VIA DELLA MATTONAIA

VIA ALESSANDRO MANZONI

Linger in
PIAZZA SANT'AMBROGIO
The area's nightlife centres around this piazza, where old friends catch up while weaving in and out of cheap bars. Hang out by the church, listening to music play and soaking up the joyful vibes.

VIA DI MEZZO

SANT'AMBROGIO

VIA PIETRAPIANA

BORGO LA CROCE

Alla Sosta dei Papi
is a popular vino sfuso *(loose wine shop), where you can get a glass of wine for €1 or fill your own bottle for €5.*

PIAZZA
CESARE
BECCARIA

4

IAZZA
DEI
IOMPI

3
Dine at
CIBRÈO
Tuck into a typical Tuscan dish at this popular trattoria. The staff are always ready with recommendations.

PIAZZA
LORENZO
GHIBERTI

2
Aperitivo at
I MACCI
Order a pre-dinner cocktail at this buzzy bar/restaurant and take it outside to Largo Annigoni to mingle with the locals doing the same.

VIA FERDINANDO PAOLIERI

VIA DELLA GIOVINE ITALIA

VIA DELL'AGNOLO

VIA GHIBELLINA

VIA DEI MACCI

1
Get a culture fix at
MAD – MURATE ART DISTRICT
See what's on at this former jail turned contemporary art space, where you might catch an exhibition, workshop or gig before it closes at 7:30pm.

OUTDOORS

People-watching in piazzas, strolling the winding streets, lazing in pretty parks: spending time outside is central to enjoying the easy-going Florentine lifestyle.

Scenic Strolls

A gentle afternoon or evening amble is so ingrained in Italian life that it's become something of a ritual: the **passeggiata.** *The best way to soak up the city is on an aimless wander through its cobbled streets.*

VIA DI SAN LEONARDO

Map 5; San Niccolò; ///promise.nitrate.manhole

The countryside is never far away in Florence: within just a few minutes of the busy centre, you can be walking down quiet rural lanes. Via di San Leonardo in the south is one such lane, hugging the old city walls beyond Forte di Belvedere. Every Florentine has at some point ambled down this winding road, picking out their dream home from the vibrant houses, glimpsing the olive groves and basking in the tranquillity before turning onto the bustling Viale Galileo.

FIESOLE

Map 6; start at Piazza Mino da Fiesole; ///lucky.healers.websites

It's a sweaty, two-hour hike to this sleepy hilltop village, 8 km (5 miles) north of Florence, so save your energy and hop on a bus instead – once you're up here, you're going to want to spend the day walking around. After all, there's a Roman amphitheatre, Romanesque

If you're here in August, head to Fiesole for the Feast Day of San Lorenzo on the 15th, to watch the fireworks over in Florence.

churches and 4th-century BC Etruscan walls to explore. As you walk up the steep cypress tree-lined lanes, stop to marvel at the view over Florence's marbled rooftops and minuscule Duomo in the distance.

PARCO DELLE CASCINE

Map 6; enter from Piazzale delle Cascine, Porta al Prato;
///pulp.spells.conclude

This rambling expanse of green fields outside the centre is where locals go to get lost in nature. The Medici's former hunting ground, Cascine Park is loved by joggers and cyclists these days, who breeze past students plugged into podcasts and parents pushing prams along tree-lined avenues. You could lose a day ambling through the acres of parkland, heady with the smell of cedar, birds flitting above.

SAN NICCOLÒ

Map 5; start on Via di San Niccolò; ///identify.bumps.cloud

A late afternoon stroll through this quaint, sleepy neighbourhood truly encapsulates Italy's *dolce vita* (sweet life) ethos. While most visitors charge up San Niccolò's maze of cobbled streets to reach Piazzale Michelangelo *(p179)*, the delight lies in the small details along the way, like the artists painting in open studios, or the waiters relaxing before *aperitivo* hour begins.

» Don't leave without looking up at the tall, colourful houses along the way, with their shutters open and flowers draping the windows.

VIA DE' TORNABUONI

Map 1; start at Piazza degli Antinori; ///exists.ends.obeyed

For those for whom the pages of *Vogue* provide blissful bedtime stories, this winding street is the magazine brought to life. It's Florence's high-fashion heart, where the window displays of luxurious brands always catch the eye. More than just a shopping street, though, Tornabuoni is a catwalk for students from the nearby Istituto Marangoni fashion school, who don their best outfits as they saunter along. As they'll likely tell you, the *passeggiata* is not a time to don your comfiest shoes, but rather one to show off your latest loafers.

ALONG THE ARNO

Map 1; start at Ponte alle Grazie; ///bandage.vanilla.sticking

Tuscan sunsets might be all the rage, but there's a real magic to witnessing the city slowly spring to life along the Arno river. Members of the historic Canottieri rowing club glide up and down the water in the early morning, a peaceful time of day shared only by florists and

Shh!

The city's nooks and crannies are bursting with sordid stories to tell, and the Dark Heart of Florence Walking Tour *(www.viator.com)* uncovers the best of them. Listen to a guide narrate lesser-known histories about Medici bloodshed and assassination attempts on a walk through the city centre at night, past famed landmarks like the Ponte Vecchio.

picture framers setting up shop along the riverbanks. As the morning rolls on and you walk from Ponte alle Grazie to Ponte Santa Trinita, more feet begin to pound the cobblestones beside you – a sign that the city has woken up, and an espresso at the bar is in order.

PIAZZA DELLA REPUBBLICA TO PIAZZA SAN FIRENZE

Map 1; start at Piazza della Repubblica; ///smelter.crush.dashes

This is the *passeggiata* Florentines roll out after Sunday lunch, in need of fresh air and a gossip. Friends meet in the centre of the square, kissing cheek to cheek before setting off towards Via del Corso. Though lined with medieval tower homes and pretty stores, this narrow street is about seeing and being seen, rating everyone's outfits and looking out for new faces. The people-watching continues once you reach Piazza San Firenze and settle in for *aperitivo* hour.

» Don't leave without stopping midway at Santa Maria dei Ricci, where an organ concert takes place every Sunday at 7pm and 9:15pm.

OVER THE PONTE VECCHIO

Map 5; start at the south side; ///coiling.cube.decks

Spanning the Arno, this medieval bridge is arguably Florence's most romantic spot for a *passeggiata*. Loved ones saunter arm in arm along the cobblestones at dusk, passing a lively scene of rose-sellers, buskers and portrait painters. It's especially enchanting when the lights along the riverbanks come on, the bridge reflecting beautifully in the water as the sun sets through the arches.

Delightful Piazzas

*Oh, the piazza: the beating heart of Italy. Life's
simple moments play out on these seductive social
hubs, where neighbours gossip, traders quibble and
artists sketch local scenes as they unfold.*

PIAZZA TASSO
Map 3; Santo Spirito; ///chop.cheeks.luggage

Sitting in the scruffy park at the centre, puffing their cigars slowly,
signori will hoarsely tell you that Tasso is what Piazza Santo Spirito
felt like 20 years ago. They'd be right. Children bellow as they pass
a basketball between them, and students bustle out of no-frills wine
bars, yet this piazza still manages to feel more tranquil than Santo
Spirito's lively nightlife square. Peace is found in the ordinary here
(and in the farmers' market, when the scent of freshly churned goats
yogurt wafts over all that cigar smoke on Thursday afternoons).

PIAZZA DEI CIOMPI
Map 2; Sant'Ambrogio; ///groomed.best.include

Simple pleasures can fast become joyless when extreme sun or
torrential rain hit a piazza. Not so at Ciompi, where the colonnade
Loggia del Pesce shelters coffee breaks and people-watching year

Ciompi was hit hard by the flood of 1966 – look out for markers up the walls of houses around the square to see how high it came.

round. Sip an espresso and witness the comings and goings on the piazza, from residents picking up fresh flowers at the florist to impatient bikers ringing their bells at people obliviously dawdling.

PIAZZA DELLA SANTISSIMA ANNUNZIATA

Map 4; San Marco; ///premiums.ruby.speaks

The mile-long queues for Michelangelo's *David* will invariably lead you to this piazza, but that's no bad thing. Some of Florence's best works of art are the Renaissance buildings that preside over it: Europe's first orphanage, well-proportioned porticoes, a Brunelleschi church. Besides, you won't find the buskers here inside the Accademia.

» **Don't leave without** getting a coffee from Un Caffè, accessed through a tiny door carved into the northern wall of the piazza.

PIAZZA SANTA CROCE

Map 2; Santa Croce; ///exhale.boat.policy

It might be one of the city's most famed squares, overlooked by its superb namesake church, but this piazza is decidedly local. Day in, day out, tired restaurant workers catch a few moments of sun, watching kids play tag as parents catch up. Come June, they're swapped out for competitors taking part in the famously aggressive Calcio Storico tournament, when locals gather to watch a mix of football, wrestling and rugby. Think Florence is all elegance? Wait for the elbowing.

PIAZZA DEL CARMINE

Map 3; Santo Spirito; ///blazers.earth.improves

If anywhere encapsulates the sentiment that piazzas are the living rooms of Italy, it's community-focused Piazza del Carmine. Time seems to slow on the cobblestones here, with childhood friends winding down for the day and neighbours putting the world to rights before tending to housework. Things get ever more cosy in the summer, when residents often bring tables, chairs, crockery and candles into the square, set to host an impromptu dinner party. Carmine is a true testament to the power of piazzas: it holds the neighbourhood together, one ceramic plate passed between friends at a time.

PIAZZA DELLA SIGNORIA

Map 1; Duomo; ///lemons.ropes.torched

Medici beheadings, Formula 1 car displays, the birth of the Florentine Republic: it's all happened in this square. For many, Piazza della Signoria is the official city centre, where convivial catch-ups are lorded over by the 14th-century Palazzo Vecchio and set to the hum of spoons clinking at the historic Caffè Rivoire (p61). Late at night, however, it feels eerily deserted. The crowds vying for a Uffizi ticket, gone. The waft of strong Italian coffee, a memory. The delight of the Italian piazza might be when it throbs with life, but there's something magical about wandering here undisturbed, only the ghosts of the city's past and the glow of the moonlight for company.

>> Don't leave without filling up your water bottle at the free fountain, which joyously dispenses not only fresh but sparkling water to thirsty passersby. How very Florentine.

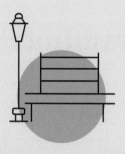

Liked by the locals

"I love the essence of piazza life in Italy, and the simplicity of being able to grab a spritz or coffee and sit under the sun catching up with friends. There's something so fun about the different energy that each piazza has, yet they're all equally magical."

CASSIDY FICKES, ENGLISH TEACHER AND
HOSTESS AT LOCALE COCKTAIL BAR

Swimming Spots

Once the summer hits, the whole city seems to evacuate the forno (oven) that Florence becomes. Lidos and lakes are a sought-after commodity, and the only way to keep cool under the Tuscan sun.

LAGO LE CERTANE
Map 6; Via Canto alle Gracchie 3, Scandicci;
///crusher.winger.undoubtedly; www.lagolecertane.com

During the winter, this artificial lake just outside Florence is a quiet slice of paradise for keen fishers. It's a different story come summer, when it turns from a members-only social club to an open-to-all lido. In the day, excitable kids play water sports while parents relax under sun umbrellas; by night, students filter in to enjoy DJ sets and karaoke competitions. It's Italian suburban summer life at its best.

LE PAVONIERE
Map 6; Viale della Catena 2, Cascine; ///onion.casually.regulate;
www.lepavoniere.it

Swerve the screaming kids who take over in the school holidays and visit this lido in June and September, when it's splash-free and the domain of chic Italians. These trendsetters don't come here to swim;

rather, they dip their feet into the water with no intention of getting wet, in part to avoid wearing unstylish mandatory swimming caps, in another to keep their new bathing suits pristine. In the middle of Cascine Park, Le Pavoniere is the ideal spot to base yourself for the day, taking sporadic dips and dozing on loungers while pop tunes play.

» Don't leave without visiting the alfresco cocktail bar, where the staff will whip you up a whisky sour.

PISCINA DI BELLARIVA

Map 6; Piscina Goffredo Nannini, Lungarno Aldo Moro 6, Varlungo; ///obey.yards.decades; 055 626 6007

For all its poolside posers, Florence is indeed home to those willing to don an unfashionable swimming cap to get their lengths in. This community can be found in the orderly lanes of this Olympic-sized outdoor pool, where the hardy brave the cold in the winter and the city's professional swim squads and water polo teams train hard.

PISCINA FLOG POGGETTO

Map 6; Via Michele Mercati 24b, Rifredi; ///sandwich.civil.jungle; www.flog.it

The FLOG complex is where Rifredi residents go to work up a sweat, following a bout of tennis or a weights session in the gym here with a dip in the outdoor pool (after an obligatory shower). If that's not you, join the students from the nearby university dorms who go straight to the pool to work on their tans. It tends to get crowded on weekends, so arrive early to claim a chair.

Solo, Pair, Crowd

A hot summer's day without the water's breeze is unthinkable in Florence. Sun yourself in peace or get splashing with the crowds.

FLYING SOLO
Sunbathe in style
Treat yourself to a day at Hidron in Sesto Fiorentino, just outside the city centre. There are two pools, a sunbathing area and even an in-house spa to get acquainted with.

IN A PAIR
A chic catch-up
You'll need to book ahead for a spot at Hotel Royal's outdoor pool in San Marco, which opens to a limited number of lucky non-guests. Once in, natter with your bestie over a cocktail as you lounge.

FOR A CROWD
Party at the pool
Easy Living – Spiaggetta sull'Arno in San Niccolò is all for the laidback vibes. Bring your gang to this bathing area on the banks of the Arno and soak up the sun while easy-going music plays.

LAGO DI BILANCINO

**Map 6; start at Bahia Cafè, Via Gastone Nencini, Barberino di Mugello;
///reflex.perches.felling**

Escaping to the sea is at the forefront of everyone's mind on scorching July and August weekends. But don't follow the majority who head to the beaches of Viareggio and Forte dei Marmi. Instead, indulge in a calmer slice of paradise and drive to the artificial Lake Bilanco, which becomes a scenic bathing spot in the summer. Of all the secluded nooks along its shoreline, the rocky beach by Bahia Cafè is a favoured hangout with nudists from the area who tan on deckchairs, and teenagers who paddleboard on the water. Spend a happy afternoon alongside them all, book in one hand and ice lolly in the other.

» Don't leave without taking a stroll around Oasi del Gabbianello, a protected nature reserve at the northeastern tip of the lake, where you'll see turtles, cranes and storks.

ASMANA WELLNESS WORLD

**Map 6; Via Salvator Allende 10, Campo Bisenzio;
///register.sleepy.wording; www.asmana.it**

No children allowed: the words every Florentine wants to hear when they're in need of a pamper. The relaxed pace of Tuscan life lends itself perfectly to a bit of R&R, and this affordable day spa – a haven of hot tubs, hammams and outdoor pools – puts it within everyone's reach. Blissed-out visitors pass days floating between the multiple areas, always pausing for a smoothie at the in-pool alfresco bar. For something extra special, visit on a Friday summer night, when the outdoor poolside restaurant hosts *aperitivo*.

Green Spaces

It can be tough to find so much as a leaf to look at among Florence's tapestry of cobbled lanes and Renaissance buildings, but patches of green do sprout here – all the more delightful for how rare they are.

GIARDINO BARDINI

Map 5; enter at Villa Bardini, Costa San Giorgio 2, Santo Spirito; ///printer.thanks.printers; www.villabardini.it

Nothing says spring has arrived like the wisteria hysteria that takes over Florence in April. The sweet fragrance never fails to tug everyone to Villa Bardini's gardens, where moments are captured under the wisteria-draped pergola, the sun casting shadows through the purple flowers. Once you've taken your obligatory photos, head to the bar at the garden's highest point for a different view of Florence.

GIARDINO DI BOBOLI

Map 3; enter at Palazzo Pitti, Piazza de' Pitti 1, Santo Spirito; ///cattle.observe.glider; www.uffizi.it/en/boboli-garden

The one-time backyard of the Medici is as grand as you'd expect. A prototypical Italian Renaissance garden, Boboli Gardens set the standard for others across Europe, with its geometric lawns, exuberant grottoes and clipped hedges. Though it's central Florence's largest green space, stretching behind the huge Palazzo Pitti, it manages to feel like your own private oasis – a place to leaf through books or picnic discreetly (blankets-out productions are frowned upon).

» **Don't leave without** checking out the Grotto di Buontalenti, where a copy of Valerio Cioli's *Fountain of the Dwarf Morgante* depicts a buffoonish court dwarf riding a turtle in the nude.

ORTI DIPINTI

Map 6; Borgo Pinti 76, San Marco; ///enjoyable.congas.scrum;
www.ortidipinti.it

Florence's alternative underbelly is all about secret green spaces like these. Built over a derelict athletics track, Orti Dipinti is the city's first community garden, looked after by a tribe of volunteers who happily toil away planting strawberries and building wooden crates. Tools are downed on Thursday evenings, when San Marco residents share compost tips over a BBQ *aperitivo*, jam sessions happen on a makeshift stage and a tarot card reader gets to work.

Try it!
GARDENING GUIDANCE

Orti Dipinti is all for local participation and encouraging sustainability. Check out the events calendar for gardening classes and workshops, or volunteer and help to build garden furniture.

GIARDINO DEL BOBOLINO

Map 6; Viale Machiavelli 18, Porta Romana/Poggio Imperiale;
///shop.bottom.cactus

Translated as "Little Boboli", and conceived as an extension of its
namesake older sibling, this quiet patch is a divine escape from the city
centre. Above Porta Romana, in the twisting roads of the Poggio
Imperiale area, yogis take to the grassy slopes and friends picnic
under huge trees without the stern looks they're likely to get at "Big
Boboli". The former Medici garden might have the renown, but
sometimes you just need a small space to journal on a quiet morning.

GIARDINO DELL'IRIS

Map 5; Viale Michelangiolo 82, San Niccolò; ///pure.warping.tinkle;
www.societaitalianairis.com

Irises – not lilies, a popular misconception – are the emblem of
Florence, and this dedicated hilltop garden is the place to see them
shine. It's open by appointment most of the year, but everyone waits

Shh!

Most locals are none the wiser
that a tiny rooftop allotment
lies above C.BIO Supermarket
(*www.cbio.it*). Buy a picnic lunch
from the deli counter and ask
for it to be put into a wicker
basket; the team will then
point you upstairs to enjoy
your food among tomato vines,
wild strawberries and roses.

until April and May to visit, when no reservations are needed to admire the flowers in bloom. The 1,500 types of iris that colour the landscape have been nurtured by the Società Italiana dell'Iris (Iris Society), largely local Italian women who enjoy getting their hands dirty. Admire their handiwork as you amble the winding paths and steal unexpected glimpses of the city below.

GIARDINO DELLE ROSE

Map 5; Viale Giuseppe Poggi 2, San Niccolò; ///teach.crate.decisive; 055 234 2426

The hilly Rose Garden makes a wonderful spot for a breather after visiting Piazzale Michelangelo *(p179)*, hidden as it is just off Monte alle Croci, the route to and from the overlook. It comes into its own during the spring, when hundreds of rose species form a pretty backdrop to couples snuggled on blankets and sunbathers relaxing.

GIARDINO DELL'ORTICOLTURA

Map 6; Via Vittorio Emanuele II 4, Rifredi; ///taps.noble.stocky; www.societatoscanaorticultura.it

It might be on the outskirts, but the Horticultural Garden always has something to lure people away from the city centre. In spring or autumn, it's the huge plant and flower showcase where locals buy plants for their homes. In August, it's the sports screenings and live music events – hard to find when the city is in its summer slumber.

» Don't leave without checking out the Art Nouveau greenhouse-terrarium, which tends to host performances and vintage markets.

Dreamy Viewpoints

There's nothing quite like witnessing the soft, Tuscan light set over Florence's terracotta rooftops and ancient church spires. For a city so small, the views are incomparably grand – whatever time of day.

OBLATE LIBRARY

Map 2; Via dell'Oriuolo, Duomo; ///burst.public.retrain; 055 261 6512

Bypass the architecture textbooks on the shelves and study the real thing at this public library: this former convent happens to have some of the best close-up views of the Duomo there are. On the top floor, the café's open-air loggia beautifully frames the orange-tiled dome and classical archways that surround it. While away the hours sipping a cappuccino here and admiring Brunelleschi's work.

SAN MINIATO AL MONTE

Map 5; Via delle Porte Sante 34, San Niccolò; ///online.forms.slogans

Piazzale Michelangelo *(p179)* may be the most famous viewpoint, but it's a well-known secret that if you hike a little further, you'll be rewarded with fewer people and better views (well, the basilica of San Miniato al Monte occupies one of the city's highest points). During the quieter winter months, many Florentines hike up here every day,

Head here at 5:30pm to hear the monks' Gregorian chanting, as they've been doing for the last six centuries.

standing on the steps to watch a golden hue paint the city and surrounding countryside. However familiar it becomes, Florence's dusky beauty never gets old.

LA TERRAZZA ROOFTOP BAR

Map 1; Lungarno degli Acciaiuoli 2r, Duomo;
///market.stripped.drill; www.lungarnocollection.com

You're paying for the view at this chic bar, where pricey cocktails accompany a front-row seat to the goings-on along the Arno and Ponte Vecchio. Perched on the fifth floor of a medieval tower turned luxe hotel, La Terrazza has fast become an "it" spot. Everyone here has an air of celebrity to them, from stylish girlfriends poised on cream couches to suave colleagues gathered around champagne buckets. Book for sunset to watch the colours fade over the Tuscan hills.

TOSCA & NINO

Map 1; La Rinascente, Piazza della Repubblica 4, Duomo;
///blushed.survey.curvy; www.rinascente.it

Forget the designer clothes inside La Rinascente department store: the real jewel is the panoramic view from its rooftop bar. Time your visit to catch the sun setting over the Duomo and the streetlights coming on in Piazza della Repubblica below, where a vintage merry-go-round and chestnut sellers make for a nostalgic scene.

» Don't leave without sharing a generous *taglieri* platter, laden with Tuscan charcuterie, cheeses, bread and olives.

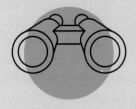

Liked by the locals

"There's something timeless about climbing up to Piazzale Michelangelo at sunset to watch the city turn golden and the lights across the city slowly flicker on. It's a moment that never loses its romance."

YAEL TER HAAR, SOCIAL MEDIA SPECIALIST

ALFORNO TOWER, PALAZZO VECCHIO

**Map 1; Piazza della Signoria, Duomo; ///struts.richer.evolves;
055 276 8325**

The Medici's forefathers were just as fond of rooftop views as modern Florentines (though spying approaching invaders might have been a stronger motivating factor than sunset selfies). This town hall's 95-m- (311-ft-) high bell tower has offered some of the best vantage points over Florence for centuries – dare we say even better than the Duomo, since you'll get a grand view of the dome itself from here. It's 400 rickety steps, lit only by arrow slits and occasional windows, to get to the top, but it's worth it.

» Don't leave without checking out the replica of Michelangelo's *David*, standing proud in front of the building.

PIAZZALE MICHELANGELO

Map 5; San Niccolò; ///thanks.dripped.filled

The panoramas from this famed terrace could very well be the postcard archetype for Florence, the Duomo looming behind pastel yellow buildings and terracotta rooftops leading to Palazzo Vecchio. As the late afternoon approaches, this view draws 9-to-5ers and backpack-wearing tourists like a beacon, everyone laden with beers as they climb winding lanes to the lookout point. Follow suit and find a spot to perch, clinking your bottles to the soundtrack of an opportune busker and the hawkings of souvenir sellers. Nothing says Florence quite like watching the sun set across the ochre cityscape and green mountains beyond, with a giant bronze cast of Michelangelo's *David* looming in the car park behind you.

Nearby Getaways

Florentines are as proud of their city as they are their region, and will passionately argue that Tuscany offers the best of Italy: golden beaches, medieval villages and hot springs, all an easy drive away.

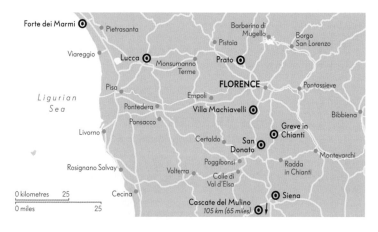

FORTE DEI MARMI

1.5-hour train ride from Santa Maria Novella station

When the heat ramps up in the summer, there's one place where the entirety of Florence's great and good decamp: Forte dei Marmi. Summering in this luxurious seaside town (nicknamed the Tuscan Riviera) is a status thing for Florentines, who endeavour to hire the same beach hut every August. Those sans beach hut still try their luck to nab an exclusive spot at the weekend, even if it means sweating in mega traffic jams and traipsing across the sand for one of the last remaining loungers. The real fun happens in the evenings, though, when sun-kissed Italians party and let loose on the beach.

GREVE IN CHIANTI

40-minute drive from Florence; www.chianti.com

The novelty of hopping on a shiny red Vespa, hair blowing in the wind as you explore the ancient wine region of Chianti, will forever be magical. The medieval market town of Greve is always the first stop – not only is it the closest to Florence, it's also the heart of the Chianti Classico wine zone. The high-quality red has been produced in the vineyards around this town for centuries, and there's no better place to have a taste than in its long-standing restaurants and wine shops.

» Don't leave without visiting Casa Ceccatelli, a historic butcher where owner Paolo will serve you cured meats with red wine.

SIENA

1.5-hour train ride from Santa Maria Novella station; www.terredisiena.it

Florence and Siena have been rivals almost as long as the two cities have existed, be it on the grounds of power, art or football. While Florentines still tend to look down on Siena as a beautiful but irrelevant little sister, visitors love the Duomo and graceful Piazza del Campo marking this Gothic brick-built town. It's a refreshing change from Florence's stately Renaissance marble.

VILLA MACHIAVELLI

20-minute taxi ride from Florence; www.villamachiavelli.it

When the parents are in town and you're scheming to keep them busy, take them to Villa Machiavelli. It's named after the mischievous Medici advisor who exiled himself here in the 16th century while writing *Il Principe* (The Prince), and remnants of his life remain today. Peek in the library where he put pen to paper, sup in the Albergaccio tavern – the oldest restaurant in Tuscany – where he'd feast, and stroll the vineyards while you plot more ways to keep your guests entertained.

SAN DONATO

45-minute drive from Florence; www.chianti.com

We know San Gimignano has it all – frescoed churches, stone towers, terraced vineyards – but the famed medieval town is always overrun with tourists. Go off-piste to San Donato instead, a Chianti wonderland almost too perfect to be true. Spying this hilltop walled village from the road is as enchanting as driving up to its little streets and piazza, where locals spill out to watch the football and share gossip.

Try it!
FORAGE FOR FOOD

Book a morning with qualified local forager Franco Lodini *(rose@artviva.com)*. He'll take you into the hills near San Donato, where you'll forage for your own herbs and edible leaves and flowers.

CASCATE DEL MULINO

3-hour drive from Florence; www.lecascatedisaturnia.com

Tuscany isn't all winding roads and rolling vineyards. The southern area of Maremma, rich in wild thermal pools, is a case in point. Italians have soaked away aches and stresses at the steaming Cascate del Mulino for millennia, so follow the smell of sulphur to join them in the mineral-rich, turquoise water. It's the perfect antidote to a chilly winter day.

LUCCA

1.5-hour train ride from Santa Maria Novella station; www.turismo.lucca.it

It can be hard to find a flat city in a region of hilltop villages and steep roads. Lucca, however, is such a rarity, and is a haven for cyclists who pedal along its ancient Roman streets. Those without two wheels prefer to take a leisurely walk around the city walls, looking down on some of the 100 churches and bustling piazza.

PRATO

15-minute train ride from Santa Maria Novella station

This suburban town might live in Florence's shadow, but it's just as dynamic as its neighbour. Florentines love spending the odd Saturday here, visiting the latest exhibition at the Luigi Pecci Contemporary Art Center, popping into local boutiques and picking up *biscotti di Prato* for the journey home.

» Don't leave without visiting the Museo del Tessuto, a museum that celebrates Prato's pioneering Italian textile heritage.

**Stroll across the
PONTE ALLE GRAZIE**

Enjoy the views over the Arno
valley and to the Ponte Vecchio
from the city's longest bridge.

1

**Pit stop at
FORTE DI BELVEDERE**

Order a coffee and relax at Florence's
largest fortress, overlooking Boboli
Gardens. If it's summer, look out for
the art sculptures that dot the grounds.

3

2

**Explore the
VILLA BARDINI**

Walk the winding Costa San Giorgio
to this 17th-century villa and amble
through the beautiful gardens.

6

**Relax over dinner at
LA BEPPA FIORAIA**

Breathe in the perfumed
air at this pretty garden
restaurant, nibbling on
sharing platters and pizza.

**Meander along
VIA DI SAN LEONARDO**

Backing onto the medieval old walls, this is
one of the city's most picturesque streets.
Admire the olive groves and grand houses
as you go, picking out your dream home.

4

*Famed composer
Tchaikovsky wrote* Third
Suite for Orchestra *at*
**Via di San Leonardo
64.** *A plaque here
honours his stay.*

0 metres   250
0 yards   250

*Ponte
Santa Trinita*

PIAZZA
DEL GRANO

PIAZZA
SANTA CROCE

VIA DEI BENCI

*Ponte
Vecchio*

VIA MAGGIO

VIA GUICCIARDINI

COSTA SAN GIORGIO

VIA DEI BARDI

Arno

PIAZZA
DEI PITTI

PIAZZA N.
DEMIDOFF

LUNGARNO
SERRISTORI

VIA SAN NICCOLÒ

VIA DEL MONTE ALLE C

*Giardino
di Boboli*

VIA DI SAN LEONARDO

VIALE   GALILEO

VIA N. MACHIAVELLI

VIALE   GALILEO

*Built in 1324, **Porta San Niccolò** was once part of a gate in the defensive walls that surrounded Florence, allowing access into the city.*

PIAZZA
G. POGGI

PIAZZALE
MICHELANGELO

VIALE MICHELANGIOLO

VIALE GALILEO

5

Go misty-eyed at
**SAN MINIATO
AL MONTE**

Watch the Tuscan sun paint the city amber from the steps of this basilica. It's even higher than the iconic Piazzale Michelangelo.

An afternoon
south of the Arno

Gently undulating hills and winding roads lined with cypresses aren't reserved for Tuscan towns: such a dreamy landscape exists on Florence's southern hillside too. Few people venture this way, though, favouring the northern town of Fiesole for their countryside walks. Savour the serenity on this beautiful stretch of land, passing remnants of the old city walls and soaking up the best views over the city. Word to the wise: wear your trainers, as it can get pretty steep at points.

1. Ponte alle Grazie
Lungarno delle Grazie
///strut.himself.palace

2. Villa Bardini
Costa San Giorgio 2, San Niccolò; www.villabardini.it
///printer.thanks.printers

3. Forte di Belvedere
Via di San Leonardo 1, San Niccolò; www.cultura. commune.fi.it
///pebble.revise.riper

4. Via di San Leonardo
///recipient.stressed.single

5. San Miniato al Monte
Via delle Porte Sante 34, San Niccolò; www.san miniatoalmonte.it
///online.forms.slogans

6. La Beppa Fioraia
Via dell'Erta Cantina 6r, San Niccolò; www.beppa fioraia.it
///mammal.declining.clothed

Porta San Niccolò
///info.paradise.gross

Via di San Leonardo 64
///data.suppers.altering

With a little research and preparation, this city will feel like a home away from home. Check out these websites to ensure a healthy, safe stay in Florence.

Florence

DIRECTORY

SAFE SPACES

Florence is generally inclusive and welcoming. Since it's a small city, though, there aren't as many organizations operating here as in other European cities. Nonetheless, should you feel uneasy or want to find your community, there are supportive spaces to turn to.

www.arcigayfirenze.it
Centre running events and offering support for the LGBTQ+ community.

www.artemisiacentroantiviolenza.it
Women's association offering psychological help and legal support for victims of violence.

www.firenzebraica.it
Jewish community centre hosting festivities like Shabbat and providing information on kosher spots in Florence.

www.ireos.org
Volunteer-run association providing services for the LGBTQ+ community.

www.unobravo.com
Online therapy centre offering mental health support, available in English.

HEALTH

Healthcare in Italy isn't free so take out comprehensive health insurance; emergency healthcare is covered by the European Health Insurance Card (EHIC) for EU residents and the UK Global Health Insurance Card (GHIC) for those from the UK. If you do need medical assistance, there are many pharmacies and hospitals across town.

www.doctorsinitaly.com/florence
Private clinic connecting you with English-speaking doctors 24/7.

www.farmaciecomunalifirenze.it
*Pharmacy with various branches open
24/7, including at weekends.*

www.salute.gov.it
*Italy's Ministry of Health, offering
general advice and information on
the nearest hospitals and clinics.*

www.uslcentro.toscana.it
*Official portal for healthcare in Tuscany,
with information on local clinics.*

TRAVEL SAFETY ADVICE
Before you travel – and while you're
here – always keep tabs on Italy's
latest regulations and security measures.

www.esteri.it
*The Italian Foreign Ministry government
portal, offering the latest information
on security and regulations, including
updates on COVID-19 travel.*

www.feelflorence.it
*Florence's Tourism Bureau, with lists
of useful numbers, consulates and
information points.*

www.poliziadistato.it
*The civil branch of the police force, with
information on staying safe, emergency
service numbers and reporting crimes.*

www.visittuscany.com
*Tuscany's official tourism website,
with useful numbers and up-to-date
information on COVID-19 regulations.*

ACCESSIBILITY
While museums and transport services
have improved enormously when it
comes to accessibility, Florence's
cobbled streets prove tricky for those
with reduced mobility. These resources
make exploring the city easier.

www.disabili.com
*Tips and resources about accessible
travel in Italy, including a list of accessible
museums and sites in Florence.*

www.moveris.it
*Arranges tours and services for travellers
with specific requirements.*

www.rfi.it
*The Italian railway infrastructure, Rete
Ferroviaria Italiana (RFI), with information
on getting help at railway stations,
including Santa Maria Novella station.*

www.toscana-accessibile.it
*Tuscany's official website for accessibility,
providing region-wide information on
accessible services, transportation, hotels
and attractions.*

INDEX

ABOUT THE ILLUSTRATOR

Mantas Tumosa

Creative designer and illustrator Mantas moved from his home country of Lithuania to London back in 2011. By day, he's busy creating bold, minimalistic illustrations that tell a story – such as the gorgeous cover of this book. By night, he's dreaming of adventures away, catching up on the basketball and cooking Italian food (which he can't get enough of).

Main Contributors Vincenzo D'Angelo, Mary Gray, Phoebe Hunt

Senior Editor Lucy Richards

Senior Designers Tania Gomes, Ben Hinks, Vinita Venugopal

Project Editor Zoë Rutland

Designer Jordan Lambley

Proofreader Stephanie Smith

Senior Cartographic Editor Casper Morris

Cartographer Ashif

Cartography Manager Suresh Kumar

Jacket Illustrator Mantas Tumosa

Jacket Designers Tania Gomes, Jordan Lambley

Senior Production Editor Jason Little

Senior Production Controller Samantha Cross

Managing Editor Hollie Teague

Managing Art Editor Sarah Snelling

Art Director Maxine Pedliham

Publishing Director Georgina Dee

A NOTE FROM DK EYEWITNESS

The world is fast-changing and it's keeping us folk at DK Eyewitness on our toes. We've worked hard to ensure that this edition of Florence Like a Local is up-to-date and reflects today's favourite places but we know that standards shift, venues close and new ones pop up in their place. So, if you notice something has closed, we've got something wrong or left something out, we want to hear about it. Please drop us a line at travelguides@dk.com

First edition 2022

Published in Great Britain by Dorling Kindersley Limited, DK, One Embassy Gardens, 8 Viaduct Gardens, London SW11 7BW, UK

The authorised representative in the EEA is Dorling Kindersley Verlag GmbH. Arnulfstr. 124, 80636 Munich, Germany

DK Publishing, 1745 Broadway, 20th Floor, New York, NY 10019, USA

Copyright © 2022 Dorling Kindersley Limited
A Penguin Random House Company
22 23 24 25 10 9 8 7 6 5 4 3 2 1

A CIP catalog record for this book is available from the British Library.
A catalog record for this book is available from the Library of Congress.
ISSN: 1542 1554
ISBN: 978 0 2415 6850 7
Printed and bound in China.
www.dk.com